ASHES TO ACTION

FINDING MYSELF AT THE INTERSECTION OF THE MINNEAPOLIS UPRISING

SHARI SEIFERT

MOUTH HOUSE

AMPLIFYING VOICES FOR CHANGE

Cover image: Volunteers clean up trash, debris after Minneapolis riots over George Floyd's death. Copyright © Getty Images Plus via Getty Images. Used by permission. Interior image: Ella Endo. Copyright © Ella Endo. Used by permission of the artist. Mouth House Series Editor: Dawn Rundman
Cover design, series design, interior design, and typesetting: Tory Herman
Project Management: Julie O'Brien

Print ISBN: 978-1-5064-9678-8
eBook ISBN: 979-8-8898-3207-2

Manufactured in the U.S.A.
28 27 26 25 24 23   1 2 3 4 5 6 7 8 9 10

Editor's Note: Text messages and social media posts are lightly edited for punctuation.

This book is dedicated to those that are starting to do the work of racial justice in our churches and in the world. May we be continually curious learners and become good ancestors.

All royalty payments received from the sale of this book will be donated to George Floyd Global Memorial. One way we can help keep history from being whitewashed is to have Black community members tell the story. George Floyd Global Memorial does an amazing job, and it is my honor to support their work. I encourage you to check out George Floyd Global Memorial and to make a donation as well.

CONTENTS

FOREWORD

The murder of George Floyd on May 25, 2020, a block away from Calvary Lutheran Church in south Minneapolis, would bring about a time of transformation born out of tragedy for this congregation and the surrounding neighborhood.

Through the leadership of Shari Seifert and others, this particular congregation responded faithfully.

But the situation could have gone another way. Amidst the global pandemic, the Calvary community could have shuttered our building and retreated from action. Or we could have made the mistake of responding in a way that would create suspicion among our neighbors had we tried to stand out instead of standing with them.

Like many small but mighty urban congregations, Calvary has a long history of engaging with the neighborhood. In its more recent history, Calvary began the challenging work of striving for racial justice in a new way. A strong group of leaders, who you'll read about in these pages, insisted that we could no longer limit our work to organizing and advocating. We needed to prioritize intentional self-reflection *and* congregational reflection. Racial healing comes about not by minimizing for fear of experiencing shame or guilt, but by honestly learning from our past and listening to our sisters and brothers who continue to suffer from racial injustice.

All of this surely played some role in the approach that we took to this tragedy. We began not by putting together a plan to take charge of something, but by simply showing up, listening, and gently asking, "What is needed of us in this moment?" It was clear from the beginning that our role would be to accompany and support those leading this neighborhood response.

We were unwittingly thrust into this new experience of "church" where it became nearly impossible to distinguish the people of the congregation from the people of the neighborhood. We didn't pull them in—they pulled us out.

We learned empathy and practiced God's mission not by tactical planning but by listening to the stories of others.

As you will see from her personal story, Shari Seifert has been at this work for a long time. We were fortunate that the elected leaders of the congregation trusted Shari and many others to lead what we could only hope and pray would be an appropriate response to this tragedy.

Martin Luther King Jr.'s vision of the beloved community continues to shape what it means to be the church today. Shari's use of this image is powerful in its aspiration—it's both now and not yet!

The tragedy of George Floyd's murder provides a jumping off point for us all to reflect on what it means to align ourselves with our neighborhoods and the work of dismantling white supremacy. When this work makes us uncomfortable, that's okay. As people of faith, we trust that even in the midst of suffering, death, and our own vulnerability, God brings about new life.

Rev. Hans Lee
Pastor at Calvary Lutheran Church, 2018–2022

CHAPTER 1

MAY 26, 2020

On May 26, 2020, at 2:28 a.m., a friend sent me the video of George Floyd's murder in Minneapolis, Minnesota. I happened to wake up in the middle of the night, and I watched the video without knowing what it was. Sadly I was not shocked. I was *horrified*. I learned the murder happened in south Minneapolis at 38th Street and Chicago Avenue, one block from my church at 39th Street and Chicago—Calvary Lutheran Church.

I knew I needed to jump into action.

I pleaded the following on my Facebook page that day:

Trigger warning—murder by police on video

I am outraged and heartbroken. I just learned that the Minneapolis police murdered a man one block away from my church. We do not need to wait for more information to be outraged, it is all on video. The official Minneapolis Police Department statement was that there were no weapons used and that the man suffered a "medical condition." Yeah, he died because the police officer kept his knee and weight on this man's neck while the man begged them to stop and kept saying "I can't breathe." All the while another police officer just stands by. I call that knee a weapon. This can't be swept under the rug—we have video.

And f*ck white supremacy. We all know the Minneapolis police keep electing a white supremacist as the head of their union. WTH. And church—we have to talk about our role in keeping white supremacy in place. How many of us have white Jesus in stained glass or in paintings on our church walls? We know Jesus was a brown-skinned Palestinian Jewish man executed by the state. How many of our churches use *white* to equal "good" and *black* to equal "evil"? White Lutherans—we need to stop trying to make God in our image and start really seeing Jesus. Part of the body of Christ was just murdered one block from our church—we need to commit ourselves to rooting white supremacy out of ourselves and our church. How else besides white supremacy can you explain the police so callously taking this man's life while he cried out for his mom.

Absolutely horrifying. Again.

Protest today—38th and Chicago, 5:00–7:00 p.m. Wear a mask and keep a safe distance.

Then I sent an email to people connected with Multifaith Anti-Racism, Change, & Healing (MARCH) to alert this network of faith-based anti-racist activists about the event and the protest march.

Hi—Could someone send out an email to ask folks to show up to the protest today at 5:00 p.m. at 38th and Chicago? This is *one block* from Calvary. A group of folks are going to meet in the Calvary parking lot at 4:30 to *try* to mark some spots to stand with chalk in hopes of helping with social distancing. Come if you can, and bring chalk if you've got some. I am assuming you have heard the news that the MPD straight up murdered another black man. I advise not watching the video—it's awful.

As a member of the European Descent Lutheran Association for Racial Justice (EDLARJ) board, I also connected with board members to craft this statement:

May 26, 2020, Statement by EDLARJ

Ahmaud Arbery, Breonna Taylor, and George Floyd are our neighbors, as are those who have gone before them. Ahmaud Arbery was lynched by a retired police officer and his son while jogging in Brunswick, Georgia (February 23, 2020). Breonna Taylor, a twenty-six-year-old American emergency medical technician, was shot eight times by Louisville Metro Police Department officers who entered her apartment in Louisville, Kentucky, while serving a "no-knock warrant" (March 13, 2020). George Floyd was killed by police in Minneapolis, Minnesota, last night (May 25, 2020) while begging for his life, only a block from one of our ELCA [Evangelical Lutheran Church in America] congregations, Calvary Lutheran Church. We declare that this is a sin, and that we, as a mostly white church, must repent of our history of racism, as well as our current biases.

In Matthew 22:37-39, Jesus [says]: "'Love the LORD your God with all your heart and with all your soul and with all your mind.' This is the first and greatest commandment. And the second is like it: 'Love your neighbor as yourself.' All the Law and the Prophets hang on these two commandments."

As the European Descent Lutheran Association for Racial Justice (EDLARJ), we condemn the white supremacy that has led to the deaths of so many unarmed Black neighbors in our country. These lynchings are nothing new. We are weary of knowing we are complicit in these murders. But our weariness pales in comparison to the trauma of our Black neighbors. We must, as a church, get to work on dismantling white supremacy. Our siblings are dying around us from our lack of willingness to truly repent of not loving our neighbors as ourselves.

In the comment section of this post are books you can read, websites you can visit, and tips for starting or deepening your own commitment to caring for our neighbors, as Jesus commands.

In addition to these communications immediately after George Floyd was murdered, I also worked to help support the first protest.

The person who had sent me the video of George Floyd's murder was an organizer of this first protest. We talked about using Calvary's parking lot as the launching place for the protest. A call to Pastor Hans Lee yielded a quick "YES!" to this request.

Unfortunately, we are very used to protests in Minneapolis. A well-oiled machine quickly and nimbly jumped into action. Marshalls showed up first in yellow vests. Calvary members showed up in a variety of ways. Some organized nurses to provide medical care if needed. Some set up tables. Some marched. Some carried the Calvary church's banner. Some showed up with facemasks. Some picked people up at the end of the march at the Third Precinct. The broader community *really* showed up with mountains of food and water, and thousands showed up to march on May 26. Those unaccustomed to protests in Minneapolis were shocked by the turnout and the supplies offered. It was like loaves and fishes.

As people gathered, the emotions were high, people were on edge, and things felt very tense. I sensed electricity moving through my body and was hypervigilant. Not only did our city just witness a brutal and callous murder by the Minneapolis Police, we were also in a global pandemic. Being around a crowd seemed risky—I felt a little uneasy, but staying away was not an option.

I had to show up and say "Enough! *Basta!* This has to stop! We're not doing this any more!"

This was a time when I had been visiting very few people in person because of COVID-19. I was grateful and reassured when I saw people that I knew.

I had no idea that the protest would become global. Given the conviction I felt from the crowd, though, the response from around the world should not have been surprising.

As we gathered to march, at one point we heard a deafening squeal of engines. I was afraid that we would get run over. Nationally, in recent protests there had been too many instances of counterprotesters using their cars as weapons and killing people in the street. The crowd and I quickly ran to the sidewalks to try to escape danger. After I caught my breath, I could see that the sound was coming from fellow protesters who showed up on motorcycles. They were here to say "Enough!" too.

I started out with the crowd when the march began, but decided I needed to stay back at the church. I took note of Calvary members who marched with our banner and felt responsible for their safety. After all, I had invited them to attend this protest—I wanted them to come out okay. But instead of going with them, I felt drawn to monitor the march that was still leaving the church and to keep tabs on it until it ended.

A range of Calvary folks were there: new members, people on our Race Equity Committee, and youth from our church that I have known since I met them as newborns in the hospital.

At the end of the evening I called to make sure that everyone had made it safely home. My wife Melissa drove some people to Calvary from the Third Precinct. At this time in the pandemic, people were cautious about riding in a car together, but the protest attendees made it work, and everyone from Calvary got home safely.

When the march was over that night, I thought that would be the end of it.

Sadly, we have seen the death of many black men at the hands of police departments in the Minneapolis–Saint Paul metropolitan area with no accountability. After Philando Castile's death in Falcon Heights, Minnesota, in 2016 was caught on video and there was no accountability for the cop who killed him, it seemed that justice would never come. Ever. The community was outraged that Philando, a beloved community member who was pulled over for a broken taillight, who fed children in a Saint Paul school, who had rainbows in his heart, was killed by a cop, and that police officer was found to be not guilty. Actually having a trial was an improvement, but the "not guilty" verdict felt like business as usual. Yes I was jaded, numb, outraged, and lacking in hope. I believe the depth of my emotions were a small fraction of what was being felt by Black people in the community who have understood and felt the realities of extrajudicial killing of Black people far longer and more intimately than I have.

Clearly things did not end that May 2020 night after the march to the Third Precinct in my neighborhood—the precinct of Derek Chauvin, Thomas Lane, J. Alexander Kueng, and Tou Thao, the Minneapolis Police Department officers who were responsible for the death of George Floyd.

Protesters angry at the lynching of George Floyd gathered in large numbers outside of the Third Precinct. Police officers responded violently, shooting tear gas at peaceful protesters. Things escalated from there. The people Melissa picked up from the Third Precinct later reported that the cops had started shooting tear gas before she arrived.

It seemed the cops weren't holding anything back.

CHAPTER 2
THE FIRST WEEK

The week following the murder of George Floyd was a fear- and anger-filled mix of dramatic violence, crumbling infrastructure, and disconnection, but also a time of connection, kindness, and generosity. It was a surreal, scary, and holy time to live through.

I did not get much sleep that week.

In addition to dealing with what was happening in the city, I was also tending to the needs of my real estate clients.

And our son's high school announced the immediate end of the school year, so there would be no school on Tuesday, May 26. School administrators encouraged the kids to focus on taking care of themselves. They said that teachers and other professionals would be available if students wanted to process what was happening in our city.

Although the days felt relatively calm, the nights brought more fear and chaos, especially in certain pockets of metropolitan Minneapolis and Saint Paul. In south Minneapolis, the intersection of 38th Street and Chicago Avenue remained a fairly peaceful place of reverence, as many people showed up to witness the spot where George Floyd took his last breaths and to pay their respects.

The area around the Third Precinct building remained a hot spot for several days. We live less than two miles away on a block of single-family, owner-occupied homes with detached garages. One evening later that week, we met with our neighbors to talk about how we could keep each other safe.

Everyone agreed to put garbage, recycling containers, grills, propane tanks, and anything flammable in our garages. (We later learned that similar conversations were happening all over the city.) We attached nozzles to hoses, turned the water on, and pulled hoses to front yards so that anyone could use the hose if needed. We regularly checked around our houses and garages for "placed flammables," because these had been found elsewhere in the city.

One young neighbor suggested blocking off our street and not allowing any traffic through. Another neighbor who had retired from special forces duty discouraged this action. Instead, neighbors took turns watching our streets and developed text communication loops with their closest four to six houses. We were all stocked up with plenty of food and water. We were as ready as we could be if our block experienced fire, gunfire, power outages, phone/communication outages, or needing to be on lockdown in our houses for a few days.

I was struck with how gentle neighbors were with one another during this vulnerable time.

At night our city was on fire. In the mornings we could see the ashes—sometimes in our backyards. The Third Precinct headquarters burned. Most buildings around it burned or were severely damaged, including the local Target store, large grocery stores, the post office, the public library, several immigrant-owned businesses, the Wendy's restaurant, an apartment building under construction, small businesses, and an AutoZone store. Amazingly, the homes people lived in were spared.

The fire department did not respond to the fires. Not to any of them.

I remember being up late one night and seeing my state senator Patricia Torres Ray pleading on Facebook for the fire department to respond. It was horrifying that firefighters never came and deeply disturbing that this trusted emergency service just didn't show up. The Minneapolis Police Department has proven themselves to be unreliable at best, but I have always taken comfort in the protection of the fire department. To my knowledge, no one has ever said "F*ck the fire department."

Metro Transit suspended all services on Thursday, May 28. This meant that the buses and light-rail train would no longer be running through our community because of the ongoing riots and protests. (In the context of the Minneapolis uprising, I refer to *riots* as actions by local and outside agitators and/or white supremacists that were meant to destroy basic infrastructure and/or to start a race war. *Protests* were carried out by people outraged by the murder of George Floyd. In my experience it was a common way of distinguishing between groups with different intent during the first weeks of the uprising.) Cutting off these public transportation services meant that thousands of people couldn't get to work, to medical appointments, or to grocery stores or pharmacies. It was devastating and created an atmosphere of scarcity.

The Minnesota National Guard arrived on Thursday. Seeing armored trucks rolling down our city streets added to the surreal nature of the landscape of our city. I remember hoping that the National Guard would help get the

Minneapolis Police Department under control. Instead, I was disappointed to hear reports of the National Guard shooting marking rounds at people who sat on their own front porches. Marking rounds are less powerful cartridges or bullets that have a plastic tip and paint at the end.

That Thursday evening we visited with our dear friends Jane and Mary in their backyard. I was in my eleventh week of working from home after Governor Tim Walz issued a stay-at-home order on March 25 in response to the COVID-19 virus. Our family was used to seeing these steadfast friends on a regular basis, but the pandemic had disrupted this pattern. Seeing these friends in the midst of the chaos was reassuring. At least we could feel some kind of normalcy.

We quickly learned from on-the-ground reports from friends in Minneapolis that other neighbors in the city were not faring as well. Because grocery stores, pharmacies, and transportation were now unavailable, people without much money or many resources were struggling get food and other necessary supplies. (During the pandemic I began ordering groceries online and picking them up at a suburban grocery store in my reliable car. I could continue to obtain food, toilet paper, and other needed supplies; my family would not run out.) We didn't know how long these disruptions to transportation and food supplies would last.

Minnesota is known for welcoming refugees from several countries due in part to the work of Lutheran Social Service in Minnesota. In Minneapolis, we are blessed with many immigrants who were refugees. I imagine that the unrest in Minneapolis could retraumatize these new Minnesotans who had left war-torn countries.

On Friday via email, I called a rapid response video meeting for Calvary people at 11:00 a.m.:

> Hi—so sorry for the late notice—things are very fluid. For those that can join, we will have a Zoom at 11:00 today—I am planning on an hour or less to discuss response from Calvary in the current time. On the agenda:
>
> › organizing medical folks/nurses to be present at medic sites
> › helping to keep information current
> › potential for Calvary to become a medic site
> › creating a banner/sign to hang outside Calvary
> › prayer vigil—possibly with Holy Trinity [Lutheran Church]
> › food shelf—special needs?
> › other?

It was reassuring to connect with Calvary members and do some planning and thinking together.

During this meeting, at 12:19 p.m. I received a very brief email from Calvary member Judi Linder that immediately brought me to tears:

Subject line: Chauvin has been arrested, by BCA [Bureau of Criminal Apprehension].

My immediate response to Judi:

Thanks be to God!

I felt grateful and relieved. Given that the murder of George Floyd was clearly recorded on video, it may be surprising that Chauvin's arrest was a big deal. Sadly, this was an improvement over how Minneapolis police shootings had been handled in the past. A glimmer of hope caught hold in me.

My dear friend Rev. Angela Khabeb was Associate Pastor at Holy Trinity Lutheran Church at the time of the uprising. Angela is a Black woman, wife, and mother. She was deeply affected by the murder of George Floyd. Her church was just a couple of blocks from the Third Precinct and right next to the post office that had just burned. For a time Holy Trinity had been a respite spot for protesters. Then, when a nearby location hosting medics burned, those medics relocated their services to Holy Trinity.

I called Angela on May 28 and asked what was happening at Holy Trinity, what was needed, and what type of support would be helpful. She let me know about the massive amounts of food and supplies coming in, huge numbers of people who wanted "to do something," the tremendous need, and the chaos that was present. We agreed that our Calvary team could help support with communication and organization.

At 12:32 p.m. on Thursday, May 28, I sent this email to local Lutheran leaders I was connected with to create and support communication and response:

Beloveds—I am inviting you to a Zoom call at 3:30 today to discuss creating a good Rapid Response Communication system for the medic/hospitality station at Holy Trinity Lutheran Church that can also be responsive to needs lifted up by organizers. We need to create something where needs can be quickly communicated and kept current. We will also need people to manage the communications.

Agenda
› what platforms to use (Facebook pages, Google docs, Twitter)
› what needs are okay for social media
› what needs are better handled off of social media
› identifying people to help update the needs from Holy Trinity

> identifying people to liaison with organizers
> identifying people to help amplify the message

Background—as many of you know, my congregation, Calvary Lutheran Church, is one block away from where George Floyd was murdered. Calvary became the official drop-off site for the initial march. As a result of that, I and Pastor Hans (and other Calvary members) have had a steady stream of people reaching out to us with offers to help and questions about what is needed. As per usual, there are a lot of people wanting to "do something." Managing all of this is way beyond the capacity of our small but mighty congregation.

Meanwhile, the epicenter of the protest seems to be at the 3rd Precinct, which is very near Holy Trinity Lutheran Church. Holy Trinity set up a medic site and was open all night, without power, and also report[ed] experiencing people wanting to "do something" or bring something. So, it seems important to provide good communication to aid in getting helpful things to Holy Trinity and also in providing whatever communications support would be helpful to on-the-ground Black organizers and other leaders of color and to follow the lead of these organizers.

An amazing group of people showed up on the call. Some of them moved to focus on organizing in Saint Paul and others stayed focused on Minneapolis. My friends Dr. Kelly Sherman-Conroy, a Native American theologian, and Rev. Dr. Jia Starr Brown, founder of REACH Education Solutions and of Up Ministries to respond to community needs, were among those to show up and significantly support both efforts on the ground and one another.

I want to acknowledge that I was not the only one calling people together and planning. There were so many people doing this—pitching in and helping. Calling people together to plan is what I know how to do—it's my go-to strategy.

At 3:47 p.m. on Friday, May 29, I received this email from Scott Endo about some artwork his daughter Ella had created:

Ella offered this piece up for a banner or t-shirts or something.

Ella Endo grew up in Calvary and just finished her senior year in high school at the time of George Floyd's murder. She wrote about her process in creating this beautiful art: "Suddenly, I was struck by inspiration. I researched George Floyd. I dug past words about his death, and I found words about his life. Without thinking, I began drawing his face, tracing each curve and shadow until they felt familiar, and I filled the lines with words that loved ones had said about him. I drew for hours."

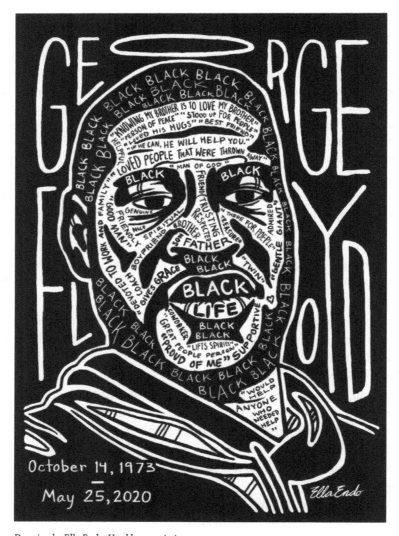

Drawing by Ella Endo. Used by permission.

On Friday, May 29, curfew started at 8:00 p.m. in both Minneapolis and Saint Paul under orders by the governor and the mayors of both cities. No one was allowed in the streets from 8:00 p.m. to 6:00 a.m. except for first responders, members of the media, and people going to and from work.

When the curfews started, my wife and I debated whether to leave the city with our family. I was concerned that things would escalate to the point of having round-the-clock curfews and ever-escalating violence. I worried it might get to the point that we would be unable to leave at any time. Melissa runs the food shelf at Calvary and was concerned about feeding people.

We stayed and rolled up our sleeves.

On May 30, the Calvary Food Shelf opened, because Saturdays were the regular distribution day. Attendance was very low. The feeling of some Calvary Food Shelf volunteers was that people were afraid to come out or perhaps thought the food shelf may not be open.

On the same day, we initiated what we now call our Community Table. We still had an abundance of food and drinks from the mountain of supplies donated for the initial march on Tuesday. We set up tables outside the church at the intersection of 39th Street and Chicago Avenue and distributed food and drinks to whoever walked by.

Sunday, May 31, was the Day of Pentecost. Pastor Hans delivered a fiery sermon. During the early days of the pandemic, Calvary held "virtual church" via videoconferencing. Typically worship participants, including our pastor and musicians, joined the online service from their own homes. During this time, we said that we were "physically distant and spiritually close." Pentecost is my favorite church festival day of worship, and so it was difficult to not be in person, especially after the week we had just been through. The service, delivered via PowerPoint slideshow and Zoom videoconferencing software, *was* very powerful, and I did feel close to my Calvary family through this service, which I watched through my tears. I felt the fiery passion and movement of the Holy Spirit during this Pentecost service. It felt like hearts were broken open and people were listening in a new way, ready for a different world.

In many ways I feel that we have stayed in a season of Pentecost when we are more in tune with our neighbors, the fiery presence of the Holy Spirit, and the call to be church in the world.

The Community Table opened after this Sunday worship service. Many people stopped by looking for groceries. Someone reached out to Melissa to let her know that people from the neighborhood were in need of food. She and others decided to open the food shelf that day too. They served fifty-three families.

On the evening of May 31, the National Guard and Minneapolis Police attacked mourners and destroyed the memorial site at 38th and Chicago.

On Monday, June 1, I joined the relief activities at Holy Trinity Lutheran Church. Holy Trinity is northeast of Calvary, located on 31st Street, near the main thoroughfare of Minnehaha Avenue. I took a break for a walk with my friend Rev. Angela Khabeb, who was Holy Trinity's Associate Pastor at that time. We walked across the street to the local bank and ATM, hoping that Angela could deposit a check. We expected the burned-out buildings and charred cars we saw on the way, but somehow held out hope that the ATM would be functional.

It was not at all functional.

We were met with a machine that had been partially dismantled and burned. We just had to laugh at the absurdity of the situation. This comic relief was welcome.

Unfortunately Angela's family lost some items that were en route in the postal system. Likely they went up in flames in the post office, which she watched burn, next door to her congregation of Holy Trinity. I imagine that many people lost precious and important items in that post office fire—checks, letters, gifts, medications, and more.

But as disruptive as all of these initial losses were—groceries, pharmacies, mail, ATMs—it was nothing compared to the loss of human life. "People over property" became a common refrain among the community of people living in the south Minneapolis neighborhoods that experienced so much loss and destruction in the days and weeks after May 25.

Beginning with that first week after George Floyd was murdered, I experienced many times when services I expected to be there were simply gone. Just like Angela and I expected the cash machine to be working, I expected "my" gas station to be there. I can't count the number of times that I pulled into "my" gas station only to remember, again and again, that it was burned to the ground. When my brother sent me a package that required a pickup at the post office, it felt jarring to remember that I didn't *have* a neighborhood post office any more. Eventually our neighborhood was redirected to a temporary post office housed in an empty Kmart store, its parking lot surrounded by a high chain-link fence. It looked bleak and felt dystopian.

Many buildings have been restored and rebuilt. However, as of spring 2023, our local post office is still being constructed and a neighborhood Walgreens pharmacy still operates out of a trailer.

I am still "people over property" all day long. The disruption is part of what helped people stop their everyday lives and pay attention to the tragedy and injustice of George Floyd's murder. I stand with those who said, "If this is what it takes to bring change, I am okay with it."

CHAPTER 3
THINGS FELT OFF

In the days following George Floyd's murder, life felt surreal, with parts of the city on fire, no public transportation, circling helicopters, burned-out stores, and the need to check for incendiary devices around our homes. In addition to that, things felt off with the protest. It did not seem like the usual crowd. I began to get suspicious when an out-of-state friend texted me that she had been watching Twitter and saw that the Boogaloo Bois, a far-right anti-government extremist group, were headed to Minneapolis and Saint Paul.

The active demonstration felt different than any other protest I had ever been a part of. It lasted longer than larger demonstrations typically do. For example, an eighteen-day occupation and demonstration in Minneapolis after Jamar Clark was shot and killed in 2015 was largely contained at the Fourth Precinct. This time, the property damage was more extensive and spread much farther than anything I had ever experienced. Basic infrastructure such as grocery stores, gas stations, pharmacies, post offices, and banks were targeted. I heard reports of pallets of bricks being delivered to places to aid in destruction. Many neighbors and friends reported seeing cars with out-of-state license plates and cars with no license plates at all. People were also driving dangerously fast down city streets.

When I wrote posts on Facebook about things feeling off to me and talking about the unusual property damage, some of my friends checked me or questioned me, because it appeared that the root of my complaint was property damage and valuing property over people. Although I did not know all the details at the time, my deep unease was rooted in the feeling that different actors with different intents were showing up and causing major disruptions. It is not unusual for some level of property damage to occur from people expressing rage at injustice at demonstrations or protests in Minneapolis.

But this was different. And I learned later that many people causing major property damage were doing so in an effort to incite a race war.

On Wednesday, May 27, "Umbrella Man" broke windows in the AutoZone store, a building that is kitty-corner to the Third Precinct building. The breaking of these windows seemed like a signal that set off more violence from white supremacists. In a July 28, 2020, *New York Times* article by Neil MacFarquhar ("Minneapolis Police Link 'Umbrella Man' to White Supremacy Group," updated on July 30), "Umbrella Man" was described in an affidavit by Erika Christensen, an arson investigator with the Minneapolis police: "The Suspect wanted to sow discord and unrest by breaking out windows and writing what he did on the double red doors."

Christensen noted that the vandalism "created an atmosphere of hostility and tension" two days after George Floyd's death. It unleashed a chain reaction of arson and looting in the Twin Cities of Saint Paul and Minneapolis, she wrote, after protests had been relatively peaceful. In a short time after the front windows were broken out in the AutoZone, looting started, the affidavit stated, noting that the AutoZone store burned down later that day. "This was the first fire that set off a string of fires and looting throughout the precinct and the rest of the city. The suspect is a member of the Hells Angels and an associate of the Aryan Cowboys, a prison gang in Minnesota and Kentucky," the affidavit stated.

During the next few days, several media outlets began reporting on the disruptive, illegal actions of people who lived outside of the community, confirming my suspicions about the involvement of different people with different intent. During a press conference held on May 29, Minnesota Governor Tim Walz discussed outside agitators. He joined the mayors of Minneapolis and Saint Paul in reporting that a majority of people arrested on Friday, May 29, were outside agitators, *not* Twin Cities residents.

Walz called those people "a highly evolved and tightly controlled group of folks bent on adapting their tactics to make it as difficult as possible to maintain order." He continued, "Let's be clear: The situation in Minneapolis is no longer in any way about the murder of George Floyd. It is about attacking civil society, instilling fear, and disrupting our great cities."

Governor Walz reported that he had mobilized more than seven hundred National Guard soldiers on Friday night and was authorizing the head of the state's National Guard to fully mobilize on Saturday.

During this press conference, Governor Walz and Attorney General Keith Ellison tried to encourage people to trust the National Guard and to distinguish between the police and the National Guard. They rightly said that people had lost trust in the police. Governor Walz said, "The very tools that we need to use to get control, to make sure that buildings aren't burned and the rule of law collapses, are those very institutional tools that have led to that grief and pain. I understand clearly there is no trust in many of our communities, and the differentiation between the Minneapolis Police Department that we witnessed losing trust of those they are there to serve is very difficult for people to make."

Attorney General Ellison added, "Don't react to them the way you might react to the Minneapolis Police Department. It's not the same group."

Of course there was good reason for community members to not trust the Minneapolis Police Department after the very public murder of George Floyd by one police officer while three others looked on. It was very clear that the violent and harmful behavior of the MPD was not limited to those four officers. During the protests, for example, Pastor Hans narrowly missed being hit by a tear gas canister, deployed by the MPD, when near the Third Precinct.

A Minnesota Public Radio story ("Ex-Minneapolis Cop Charged with Beating Man during 2020 Unrest" by Matt Sepic, December 28, 2022) reported that a former Minneapolis cop Justin Stetson was charged with beating Black man Jaleel Stallings during the first Saturday of the unrest. Stallings, a veteran with a permit, decided to bring his gun because he heard that white supremacist gangs were roaming the streets. Police shot marking rounds out of an unmarked van, and Stallings shot back not knowing who was in the van:

> "At that point, I didn't have time to speculate on who was in the van, who was shooting at me or whatnot. I had to react."

Once he realized what was happening, he surrendered with his face down on the pavement:

> According to the criminal complaint against Stetson, the former officer kicked Stallings in the head 10 seconds after Stetson "verbally acknowledged" that Stallings had surrendered. As Stallings lay face down on the pavement, Stetson kicked Stallings in the face and head at least three other times, punched him in the head "approximately six times," then allegedly lifted his head from the pavement and slammed it back down. Stallings suffered facial injuries including a broken eye socket.

Another Black man who was with Stallings, Virgil Lee Jackson Jr., was beaten and tased at the same time. We have no way of knowing how many other similar instances of police violence went unreported during this time.

The arrival of the National Guard did not bring comfort, relief, or a feeling of safety that some may expect. Both the Minneapolis Police Department and the National Guard shot marking rounds at people who were sitting on their porches. The National Guard's armored trucks and helicopters added to the surreal feeling.

Members of the media were also targeted. *The Guardian* reported that "More than fifty incidents of violence and harassment against media workers were reported on social media and in news outlets on Friday and Saturday [May 29 and 30], according to a tally the Guardian collated" ("George Floyd Protests: Reporters Targeted by Police and Crowds" by Michael Safi, May 31, 2020).

The Hubbard School of Journalism and Mass Communication at the University of Minnesota designed a photography exhibit of the reckoning that was exhibited from late October 2021 through March of 2022. I went to the exhibit and its opening night reception. It was difficult to witness the trauma represented in the photos on display.

On the exhibit's opening night, the journalism school held a reception and a panel discussion with some of the photojournalists who came from around the country. During the panel presentation and discussion, one photojournalist described covering the aftermath of George Floyd's murder as the most dangerous work they had ever done—and the danger came from the police. Some of these journalists had covered active war zones. They described creating communication loops with other journalists to help keep people safe. They weren't as concerned with getting the scoop and shooting a photo that would be picked up by multiple media outlets as they were with just keeping each other from harm.

So who *was* there during the days following May 25, 2020? I think that the protests and demonstrations were likely a mix of local people angry at the injustice of George Floyd's murder *and* opportunists who were hoping to start another civil war piggybacking on the massive protests. I suspect some of these opportunists were local, and clearly some of them were from out of state.

One of these people, a Texas man named Ivan Hunter, pled guilty to charges of riot. The US Attorney's office for the District of Minnesota reported on this case in a press release, "Self-Described Member of 'Boogaloo Bois' Pleads Guilty to Riot" (September 30, 2021):

> Ivan Hunter, 24, admitted to traveling from San Antonio, Texas, to Minneapolis with the intent to participate in a riot. Hunter is a self-described member of the Boogaloo Bois, a loosely connected group of individuals who espouse violent antigovernment sentiments. The term "Boogaloo" itself references an impending second civil war in the United States and is associated with violent uprisings against the government.

On the night of May 28, 2020, Hunter was captured on video discharging thirteen rounds from an AK-47-style semiautomatic rifle into the Minneapolis Police Department's Third Precinct building. At the time of the shooting there were other individuals believed to be looters still inside the building. Law enforcement recovered from the scene discharged rifle casings consistent with an AK-47-style firearm.

On April 5, 2022, Hunter was sentenced to fifty-two months in prison followed by three years of supervised release.

My friend was right—the Boogaloo Bois had come to Minneapolis. Boogaloo Bois were present and active in the insurrection at the US Capitol on January 6, 2021, and were arrested in the widely reported plot to kidnap Michigan governor Gretchen Whitmer. This and other extremist groups are active, organized, and focused on an objective.

White friends, we who believe in love, racial justice, and care of our neighbor need to become more active, organized, and focused. Lives depend on it.

CHAPTER 4

WE STAYED AND ROLLED UP OUR SLEEVES

Mountains of water and food remained from people's donations to Calvary after that initial march. We stored it all in the narthex. In the following days, people showed up in cars and vans overflowing with food, water, diapers, and other supplies. At one point, we had to turn away people who came bearing gifts, because the incoming donations were more than Calvary could handle.

People's generosity was truly overwhelming.

Calvary member Angie Endo encouraged us to receive *all* the gifts and find a better home for some of the offerings. She did not want to turn the people away. So we continued to receive, redistributing supplies to where they were needed, mostly in other parts of the city. We also put out calls for people to donate money and items targeted to specific needs, rather than general food and supply donations.

Even with these redistribution efforts, we still kept a large store of food and water to keep people at the site fed and hydrated. We bore witness to hundreds of people arriving to mourn at the site of George Floyd's murder.

In addition to the steady stream of visitors to George Floyd Square, large groups showed up with brooms, shovels, and garbage bags to clean up the streets. Many of them passed by Calvary. Many showed up *at* Calvary and the Square, but the Square was well taken care of by people who had already tended the area. We redirected them to Lake Street and some of the harder hit intersections.

Setting up a table outside on the corner of 39th Street and Chicago Avenue happened naturally. We had an abundance of food and water and there were many people who were hot, thirsty, and hungry right outside our doors. It just made sense to share with the community what had been shared with us.

In the first ten days or so, people spontaneously showed up to be hosts at this table. Eventually we put schedules, sign-up systems, and calls for volunteers into place. Dozens of Calvary and non-Calvary volunteers showed up regularly to host.

The table, which we began to call the Community Table, became a powerful way for Calvary folks to make connections and be a part of the neighborhood. I believe its success was dependent on its simplicity. There was no agenda, no program, and no attempts to get people to join Calvary. There were just folding tables, folding chairs, a sunshade, ice chests, and donated snacks, drinks, and masks that we gave away. Equally as important as water and snacks, we offered a "ministry of bathrooms" by letting visitors use the restrooms inside the church.

I believe a more formal approach with an agenda would have created an unequal power dynamic. We would have remained "us" and "them." We would have lost the "we" that was emerging. The setup of the Community Table created a power dynamic in which Calvary was not there to save or have "power over" in any way. It was also helpful that people who hosted the Table had time to just "be" and engage in conversation. Shifts at the Table often spanned four to six hours.

Calvary members Angie and Scott Endo and their children Lily, Ella, and Mohali were an active and steady presence at the Community Table. The Endo kids hadn't been otherwise involved at Calvary in recent years. Scott shared that their children found meaning in being there and doing things with the community outside. He reported that their kids changed the way they viewed Calvary because of the commitment they saw at the Community Table. Ella eventually designed and printed T-shirts with the George Floyd image that she had created. She sold them at the Community Table and donated all proceeds to local organizations. Ella enjoyed engaging with people about the T-shirts while they were at the table.

Angie and Scott are both teachers with summers off, and because of the global pandemic, they did not have summer travel plans. The Endos were some of the people that had plenty of time to *be* at the community table and to reflect on the significance of the effort.

When I interviewed Scott Endo in late 2022, he shared some thoughts on *serving* people versus *being in community* with neighbors:

> One of the things that . . . was surprising, but also transformational, that actually has drawn me to church, period, and to Calvary, is to not think about "church and service" as much. I think churches, including the Lutheran Church

. . . and it's probably true about a lot of churches . . . the white church is just this idea of serving the unfortunate, and it can be sort of coupled with this idea of saving or evangelizing or spreading. This idea of "We are helping people."

The Community Table was a lot about *listening* and being in community with the neighbors and *with* people who are in our neighborhood, because we're in the neighborhood, and we are residents as much as other people. We can think of ourselves as historically a pillar or an institution that is in service to its community. But you know *we* have a lot to learn. *We* have a lot to gain from our neighbors.

And so for me this was a way of living out the idea of not thinking about saving or even serving people, but being in community with people. I think being open, the transformation was possible, because I don't think we went into it with the expectation of "We're here on a mission trip."

Angie Endo described the Community Table as initially a response to trauma and the situation that later became more about community outreach that connected people and built relationships.

Angie shared about the importance of conversations with people at the Community Table in a "temple talk" on a November Sunday in 2020 during worship at Calvary:

The CT [Community Table] in its raw, basic existence exudes an amazing aura that seems to open the door to lengthy sharing. Often a visitor will talk for twenty to thirty minutes—completely uninterrupted. How often are we able to pause and just listen to a story of someone we've never met? It's empowering to simply be heard and listened to as a fellow human being.

Each time I volunteered at the Table, these conversations moved me. As labels and divisions melted away, I found myself engrossed in story, connecting on a deep human level, stirred by emotions and challenged in my thinking.

I came away enriched and consciously noticed the joy in sharing conversation with individuals that I may never have had an opportunity to meet without the Table. I realize how isolating our society can be—how so often we live parallel lives that don't overlap much at all with folks in different demographics, and when they do, it's often only on a superficial level. Within the same city, we know how white supremacy plays an integral part of that separation, as our society was built with divisions in laws and practices intended to separate. Our differences too often alienate us from others right within our midst. The Community Table broke down so many barriers that society constructs.

I often left these Community Table conversations filled with hope, insight, and even prophetic wisdom. I didn't expect this.

And through this set-up, perhaps the biggest gift offered at our Community Table is an invitation for people to talk—to share stories, experiences, thoughts—and to be heard. My time spent at the Table became sacred listening time for me. And the power of honoring each story resonated through this experience.

One of the things that I realized after engaging with people in George Floyd Square and in the neighborhood is how inadequate the phrase "Our doors are open" is as a welcome. When we say "Our doors are open," we are saying "Drop what you are doing, come in here with us, and join us in our agenda—what we already have planned without you."

Scott Endo shared his thoughts on the church "outside the walls" as I interviewed him:

> We talk a lot in church about creating welcoming space—our welcome is really about you coming from outside into our space. And I think the Community Table really flipped that. It's like "We will go outside our walls, and yes, it's a welcoming space, but it's shared space." So really, in a lot of ways we're just sharing abundance which people have shared with us in the space we're sharing with our neighbors. To me, that was so transformational and meaningful. To be communing in space that was common space for us, and not about bringing people into our space.

Both Scott and Angie pointed out that just being outside had a huge impact on how we were with our community. Here is what Angie said when I interviewed her:

> [The Community Table combined] the "us" and "them" into a "we." It was interesting, because [previously], coming to our church, we often are *inside* the building, doing all kinds of things *inside* the building, and then we leave, and then come back *inside* the building. [With the Community Table], just that stepping outside of the building, and then being in the neighborhood right there right then, for whatever was happening at whatever moment, broke down walls for us that we didn't even necessarily know existed. We thought, "Yeah, our church is part of that community." But are we as people part of that community? Are we out there and in it? Just by stepping outside the walls and having those conversations, it really did become more of a "We're with you, we're talking with you, we're getting to know you, and you're getting to know us."

OUR NEIGHBORS

The idea of Calvary members being outside making a difference was confirmed when I spoke with several people who lived near the church. Longtime neighbor Susan Heineman shared that prior to the uprising, the only person she was aware of was the "woman who did gardening" (Carol Chalman) and the evidence she saw of other congregants was cars. Neighbor Katie Dillon echoed Susan's sentiments and added that she had noticed "the procession you all do once a year" (our Palm Sunday procession through the neighborhood). Neighbor Marcia Howard shared that she didn't remember seeing the people of Calvary.

Things changed when Susan Heineman saw us outside. She shared this when I interviewed her:

> I have a friend who lives really close to the Third Precinct, and there were big chunks of ash in her yard. . . . And, she came over to my place and really to the Square at that point just to kind of decompress, and to be in a more healing space, and to be in a space that she wanted to be in, a space of grief. We were just walking through the huge crowds and flowers, and art appearing just as we went through. I remember walking down your block on Chicago, and all these folks being out by Calvary giving out water and oranges, and just kind of serving the neighborhood that way. That really was my first really big impression of what kind of congregation Calvary was, that you all were really, really out there. Between that, and also your pastor being really good about shooing police cars out of the parking lot, those were the two real turnaround moments for me.

By "shooing" police cars, Susan meant that when Pastor Hans was notified that police cars were in our parking lot, he would consistently call to let them know they were not welcome.

In my interview with neighbor Marcia Howard, she recalled being at the south barricade which was directly across the street from Calvary and the Community Table. She also described the impact of Pastor Hans shooing away the police cars.

> I do remember being on a barricade on Chicago Avenue and staring at Calvary. Quite often when there was controversy or conflict down at the south barricade, I would have to consult with the people that I was aware of from Calvary Church where it would be like "Are you all okay?" and they would come over [and ask us] "Are y'all okay?" And so it became this sort of "we were in the trenches together by proximity" and it always seemed as if we were on the same side. A lot of that had to do with the fact that Calvary, very early on, made a stand about police using their alleyway and their property to sort of stage themselves. This occurred for well over a year, and they were adamant that it was without their permission. So the cops had every right to be in the alley, but not on Calvary Lutheran Church property itself, and **they made it clear that between the protest, the community, and the cops, they were choosing community, and we were incredibly grateful.**

It is important for churches to side with the community rather than empire or the oppressive powers that be.

CALVARY FOOD SHELF

For more than thirty-five years, Calvary Lutheran Church has operated a small food shelf supporting twenty-five to thirty families weekly and operated by congregation and community member Henrietta Williams. In September of 2019, my wife, Melissa, started working alongside Henrietta to learn how the food shelf operated. After the pandemic began, Henrietta needed to step back from this work, and Melissa stepped forward.

Because of COVID-19, the Calvary Emergency Food Shelf operation moved outside for distribution. We didn't have walls anymore, so the food shelf activities became more visible and the number of families increased during the initial months of the pandemic. After the murder of George Floyd and the closing of grocery stores and public transportation, the reality of scarcity in the community soared. People couldn't buy milk or diapers at the corner store. The Calvary Food Shelf responded by adding more days for food distribution in June 2020 and then becoming more efficient at sharing more food with more families each month. We went from serving 25 to 30 families up to serving as many as 177 families weekly.

The needs of our immediate community were way beyond what Calvary alone could manage. We had neither the money nor the volunteers to do what was needed. At this time we were not worshiping in person, but "closing our doors" to the needs around us was never an option. Out of the horrific tragedy of George Floyd's death sprang amazing generosity from people near and far. Many people volunteered to help our food shelf operate, including people from the immediate neighborhood and employee groups from companies such as HealthPartners and Target. Our food shelf was even adopted for a month by the VocalEssence youth choir, Singers of This Age (SOTA), who also offered songs that we included during our online worship services.

I interviewed some staff and core volunteers of the Calvary Food Shelf, and excerpts from these conversations follow.

Amy Schroeder was one of the neighbors that stepped up and turned into a "super-volunteer" and, at times, staff. Amy started volunteering at the Calvary Food Shelf after the pandemic hit and before George Floyd was murdered. Amy shared this about her food shelf work:

> After the pandemic hit, I just got really passionate about making sure people had food. It just felt like things were so unsettling. We were having to stand in

line to go into a grocery store. You could only have so many people in a grocery store [at one time].

Amy sought out a food shelf to help and found Calvary just a couple blocks from where she lived. Amy reflected on the increased need:

> I had to go to Bloomington [a suburb about seven miles away] to go to a grocery store, and I just remember feeling very fortunate that I had a car, and I thought, "What is everybody else doing that doesn't have a car?" There was no transportation. That all shut down. I just felt like it just really made me feel like wow! We have to be there for people, because there's nothing in this neighborhood foodwise. There was a spirit of us all working together for community and for each other. I just felt that so much because I live there, so I felt like we were all in it together. Even now I get that feeling, just that heart-opening connection with everybody, just doing what we could in this really emotional time for all of us, not only dealing with the murder, but then the uprisings after.

When I asked Amy how she was transformed by the experiences at the food shelf, she spoke to that and also shared that volunteering at the Calvary Food Shelf gave her the opportunity to connect with her neighbors more deeply:

> It felt very transforming to step into that role that I was feeling called to do, and then just being a part of community. For so long, because I am a flight attendant and travel a lot on weekends, I didn't really feel part of a community. It was something I struggled with for quite a while, always trying to figure out, How can I know my neighbors better? Because I'd work a lot on the weekends, and so to come together as a community on my street, to come together as a community of volunteers at the food shelf and be part of the community for people coming to the food shelf, it just was really transforming for me in that way. And just that feeling of whenever there's catastrophe or whatever you want to call them . . . how our human spirit is that we come together and to feel like that within myself and from others around me—my immediate neighbors on my street, and then also the people at the food shelf and Melissa. Stepping up and kind of helping leading volunteers like that wasn't a role that I had really done before, and that felt very natural and good to me.

Calvary member Linda Mundt became a regular food shelf volunteer. She shared that when her son and daughter-in-law came to visit George Floyd Square on Sunday, May 31, and were at the Community Table, all of a sudden people who needed food were showing up even though it wasn't a distribution day.

> It was pretty overwhelming. There was a lot of need at that point, and obviously a lot of that initial need was because there were no stores open in our area. But the need continued. You know it's just sort of surreal when things were just

happening in real time. The need was so immediate and we wanted to help. Other than a funeral or a wedding, my son had not been in church for a good fifteen years or so. It was just sort of surreal to have him and Victoria there helping to get things ready.

Other Calvary parents shared that their "kids" became involved with the Community Table or the food shelf when they had not been involved in other Calvary activities.

The line between the Calvary Food Shelf and the Community Table was pretty blurry in the beginning. Emergency boxes of food and laundry detergent were given out at the Community Table when the food shelf wasn't open. We were just trying to meet the needs of the community. Melissa Brooks shared her thoughts about this time:

There were just so many more people asking for help, and I think before that there were probably a lot more people who needed it but didn't know where to go or didn't feel like they had the right to ask. I think our presence out on the corner made it way more accessible and way more approachable. I don't know how many of the people who came for food had had a conversation with someone at the Community Table that week, but I feel like that helped.

Melissa remembers people helping in a variety of ways:

Somebody with a farm brought eggs, and somebody's dad who worked in a bakery place where they made a lot of hot dog buns brought in a truckload of hot dog buns. People in the city were connecting with people out of the city to try to help, and it was, like Amy said, overwhelming at times. I remember the basement in the fellowship hall. A good portion of it was just covered in bags of groceries, bags of donations, and we tried to sort them out and figure out like "Okay, these are all beans, and these are all pasta." Eventually the entirety of our fellowship hall and most of our narthex was full of food and supplies for the food shelf and Community Table.

There was intentionality about making a visit to the Calvary Food Shelf a dignified experience, being culturally responsive and respectful to the customers who used the food shelf. Food shelf volunteers showed care for folks who may have had a hard time asking for help.

Linda Mundt shared this:

I think that for most people it's probably pretty hard for them to come, but they have the need and so that's why they were there. But it probably wasn't something that they had done before or needed to do before, and how humbling that we were all in it together in a way that they had a need, and we could be there to help.

Melissa responded:

I was out in the parking lot most of the time, and you're right [that] it was hard, especially in the beginning. There were people who were nervous and embarrassed, and sometimes crying and feeling like they needed to explain themselves. I just remember trying to figure out how to not totally disregard that discomfort, but to try to say, "You know, we have a lot of food. There's a lot of food in our system, and we have an abundance of food, and you're welcome to take what you need when you need it. There's abundance. You're struggling right now—you know there are a lot of people struggling right now. Don't feel bad about it. There's a lot here to share and we're trying to be more with people in the community."

Of course, the people who have used the food shelf long term were also treated respectfully!

Melissa's experience as an ESL (English as a second language) teacher informed the way that she operated the food shelf. She knew that one size did not fit all. A variety of people have a variety of tastes and needs. She described her work to create a culturally responsive environment and to maintain the dignity of those accessing the food shelf.

I think part of cultural responsiveness is just trying to understand where everybody is coming from and not make assumptions. This is something we had to work on. You know, if you've got a person of color that walks up, not assuming that they're a customer, but trying to find out "Are you a volunteer or a customer?" or "Are you donating?" I know there were several times when I put my foot in it, or heard somebody else, because most people who were coming up were customers looking for food. Just try to not make those assumptions based on how people present, or color of skin, or dress, or whatever.

Cultural responsiveness is also language and making things accessible, trying to have signs in Spanish and English, but also knowing that we had other languages and other cultures, and trying to find ways to include the food that would be welcomed by everybody. Helping people access the food. That is what they want, what they need, and avoiding assumptions that everybody should get pork, you know, because it's cheap.

Another important part of responsiveness is asking the people you're serving what they want.

Melissa said this:

I think both Amy and I and other people would say, "Is there anything that you wish you had that you didn't find?" or "How is this working for you? Do you have any ideas?" and just do what the customers suggest.

Melissa also described how debriefing after distribution days was important.

> I think for a while there after every Saturday we would have a debrief and say, "You know, this is really not working" or "People really don't like this stuff, but they want more of this stuff."

As a teacher, I was constantly reevaluating lesson plans and things. It's a lot easier for me to be open to that change than some people. Because it also brings a little bit of uncertainty like, "Well, okay, if we don't do it that way, then what are we gonna do?"

One thing I think I heard was that allowing people to ask questions, or asking people questions and having them give input and demonstrating vulnerability like that, led to improvement. And I would imagine that would lead to a less of an "us versus them" kind of dynamic and a more collaborative approach.

Amy Schroeder agreed and said:

> Also [that involved] giving power back and showing customers that they know better than we do in many situations.

During the interview with these volunteers I offered this observation:

> So this is taking a step back from paternalism.

And the group responded "Yes!"

People donated money to our Calvary Food Shelf and to our Justice Fund. Losing our walls and adopting much more permeable boundaries was truly a gift that enabled us to connect with our neighbors in a new way. We were not acting as the saviors in the situation. We were all working together for the benefit of the community.

When I had a conversation with Pastor Hans Lee about our collective experiences during the uprising, he shared some thoughts about the "missional church." It turns out that Calvary was actually doing what the missional church called for, without being cognizant of the theory or theological underpinnings.

Pastor Hans explained it this way:

> I had this evolving understanding of ministry that goes back probably ten or fifteen years about what I've referred to as the missional church movement, which is that we need to understand that the mission is not ours—it's God's mission. So what we do is try to align ourselves as the church with that mission in the world. It's not limited to what happens in the congregation. It's about showing up and participating in God's work as it happens around us and seeking to not even facilitate it as much as—it doesn't take away our agency, but it allows us to be more in our authentic presence in the community. I had that theoretical understanding of church, but it was always difficult to find ways to do that.

At Calvary, with the pandemic in the beginning when the food shelf exploded, we just kind of rallied around that and those folks that were involved. It became a community food shelf, a neighborhood food shelf, and that, to me, was like a before-George-Floyd example of how the church participates in God's mission in the world. Then George Floyd was murdered, and even though there were bumps along the way, we were able to then step in, and not because I taught you all this understanding of mission, but because you were already, without even using any kind of workbook or guide, you were actually doing that work through the race-equity work, dragging some people along—kicking and screaming, to be honest.

It was hard, but you were willing to do that, and I saw that.

Calvary had this opportunity to practice what it means to be church. I use the phrase that churches struggle with: What does it mean to be the church in mission today and going forward? **The mission of the church came to Calvary, and we participated in it.** That's how I understand that.

Not only did Calvary members participate in providing material aid in the early days, they also supported efforts to move hearts and minds by helping with an online training by the European Descent Lutheran Association for Racial Justice (EDLARJ) called "Are You New Here? Anti-racism in the ELCA" on June 10, 2020. The training centered on the Pentecost sermon by my dear friend Rev. Dr. Yolanda Denson-Byers, who preached her heart out on Pentecost Sunday. Yolanda is a queer Black woman who was pastor to a very white congregation in Minnesota during this time. The only Black members of the congregation were the ones in Yolanda's family. After the service, Yolanda reached out to me and said "Something happened. . . . I tore up my sermon and wrote a new one."

When Yolanda shared her sermon with me via video, I saw that she preached in a very raw and vulnerable way. She spoke of the fears of having Black sons. The sermon was given between verses of the Canticle of the Turning. While the stanzas were sung, Yolanda absolutely sobbed.

It seems impossible to experience this sermon and not be moved.

I believe that the way to help people understand the harm of racism in our church and in our world in a way that is going to move them to action is through their hearts. Learning the statistics about the vast number of racial disparities is important, but it often leaves white people in our heads, a place where we can rationalize and make excuses. If you get to people's hearts, though, it is easier to move them to compassion and to be open to transformation. Something that has moved me is hearing the stories of harm from my friends.

Throughout the years I have heard countless stories of harm to Arab and Middle Eastern, Asian, Black, Latiné, and Indigenous ELCA beloveds. Often these stories are gut wrenching, told in the context of deep relationship. They require significant emotional labor to tell and to hear. It is not fair to ask those hurt by our church and the world to repeat these experiences. When these stories are made public through writing or video, they provide an opportunity for learning and transformational change without as much emotional labor from those harmed.

Rev. Dr. Yolanda Denson-Byers's Pentecost sermon was so powerful. The Holy Spirit was really moving that day. I felt a larger audience should see and hear the sermon in the context of doing anti-racism work in the ELCA. We were definitely still in the season of having people's attention, so once again, I felt moved to make things happen.

I reached out to Yolanda to see how she felt about EDLARJ using her Pentecost sermon as part of a training session. We had further conversations about whether the session should be led by white folks or whether it would be better to be co-led by a BIPOC person. Ultimately we agreed that Yolanda and I would lead the training centered on Yolanda's Pentecost sermon together. We began talking about the session on June 5 and we did the training on June 10. This is a really fast turnaround for a national-level training—or any training! We were building the proverbial airplane with duct tape as we started to fly. I rounded up friends and Calvary members to be breakout room moderators, we found BIPOC folks to host break out rooms for BIPOC-only folks for people that wanted it, and I found someone from Calvary who was willing to act as Zoom administrator who was literally learning how to do that about twenty minutes before we went live. Unfortunately the capacity for the Zoom account that we were using capped at one hundred viewers, which was much lower than we thought we had capacity for. We ended up with sixty-one people who couldn't join online, so we decided to offer a second session.

I was grateful for the support from Calvary members who ran the training session and helped with breakout groups, to Rev. Dr. Yolanda Denson-Byers— it took a lot of emotional labor for her to be present for these trainings—and to ELDARJ for making this training possible. It seemed to open hearts.

CHAPTER 5
GEORGE FLOYD SQUARE

Soon after the world began to learn about the murder of George Floyd, streams of visitors came to visit the site of his death, many of the people grief-stricken and traumatized. There were also people driving dangerously fast through the south Minneapolis intersection of 38th Street and Chicago Avenue. Neighbors began putting up barricades to make the space safer for those who gathered.

The memorial started organically. Mourners brought bouquets of flowers and other offerings to the site where George Floyd was murdered. I was amazed at the memorial's beauty. In the first days and weeks, it seemed to look different every day that I visited. Flowers would be arranged in beautiful circles or sometimes hanging from powerlines overhead. I quickly learned about the caretakers who maintained the memorial. Everything brought was considered an offering, so everything was preserved. The caretakers said that the people were more important than the offerings, and they would often also spend time caring for visitors.

Eventually the city placed large concrete structures called Jersey barriers to serve as barricades at the four points before 38th Street and Chicago Avenue intersected. Eventually this closed-off intersection would come to be known as George Perry Floyd Square. Community members added a swinging gate on wheels by the concrete barriers so residents who lived within the Square and emergency vehicles could access it. People were stationed at these gates around the clock.

For many months, volunteers posted at the four entrances provided hand sanitizer and masks and offered suggestions to visitors for how to enter the space respectfully. Before the first winter, guard shacks built at each entrance warmed the people who kept vigil overnight.

Anna Barber and Connor Wright, two artists who were students at the University of Pennsylvania, designed a temporary art installation called "Say

Their Names" in the drainage field adjacent to the north end of George Floyd Square. They placed grave markers for Black folks who had been violently killed, including Sandra Bland, Emmet Till, and, of course, George Floyd. The artists did not expect the installation to last, but this area continues to be tended to by community members. The artists returned at the first commemoration of George Floyd's death and added more markers to what is now the Say Their Names Cemetery.

People have offered an abundance of powerful art to the memorial. Jordan Powell-Karis, a local community artist, built a large power fist statue out of wood that was placed in the middle of the intersection. This wooden fist was eventually replaced by the artist with a more permanent metal fist, and smaller fists were placed at the four entrances into the Square. An abundance of flowers and vegetables appeared throughout the Square. Youth painted several planters that are brought out during the warm months and kept in the Square greenhouse so that the plants in them survive the winter.

Another artist painted "the mourning passage" or the "street of names" on the south portion of Chicago between the fist statue and 37th Street. The names of beloved Black folks lost mostly to police violence are written on the pavement of this street.

The area where George Floyd's body lay while he was being murdered was cordoned off. A mural was painted near the site of his death. Additional murals have been painted in the same spot as the previous murals were worn away by weather and the elements.

For me, this cordoned-off area is the place where I most often feel the deepest grief and sadness. When I enter into this space, it feels similar to how visiting the memorial to Emmett Till in the Smithsonian's National Museum of African American History and Culture in Washington, DC, felt to me.

The mayor of Minneapolis wanted to remove the concrete barricades a few months after they had been placed. Some people thought there had been adequate time to mourn. The city was told by community members that the barriers could not be moved until we had justice. Community member Jeanelle Austin communicated in a private conversation, "Injustice closed these streets, only justice should open them." Community member Marcia Howard began chanting the phrase, "No justice, no streets."

These sentiments were presented to the mayor in their first meeting. The community has stood by "Injustice closed these streets, only justice should open them." "No justice, no streets" has been the refrain of the community for months (and now years). The city asked what justice looks like. Marcia Howard and Jeanelle Austin talked to neighbors and business owners about what justice looked like to them and were eventually joined by community member Madi RT in this effort. The responses from the neighbors and business owners were assembled into the 24 Demands which were signed by Jeanelle Austin, Marcia Howard, and Madi RT prior to being sent to the city. (This statement can be accessed online through a search for 24 Demands.)

The concrete barricades placed by the city stayed for about a year, and their removal was controversial. Calvary's Community Table was directly across the street from the south barricade. The Bahá'í Center of Minneapolis was adjacent to the north barricade, and its members have also been active as community members of George Floyd Square. Marcia Howard has said that Calvary and the Bahá'í Center have been two tent poles that have helped keep the Square dry.

George Floyd Square is multiple things at once.

It is an active site of protest.

It is a memorial site where people come to pay respects and grieve.

It is part of a neighborhood.

It is a community of people.

Whole libraries could be written about George Floyd Square. Many of the stories are not my stories to tell. I will just mention a few things.

"Meet in the Street" started on June 15, 2020, as a way for neighbors to connect with one another. Pastor Hans told me about this meeting so I decided to check it out. "The neighbors just meet in the streets," he said. One of the people I saw at Meet in the Street was Marcia Howard, one of my son's favorite teachers from Roosevelt High School, who is also a neighbor. I was glad to see someone there I had previous connection with. This group initially met every day at 8:00 a.m. and 8:00 p.m. When the days started getting shorter, the evening meeting time moved to 7:00 p.m.

As of this book's publication, the meetings have been ongoing for more than 1200 days. We continue to meet daily at 8:00 a.m. and 7:00 p.m. in the parking lot of an abandoned Speedway gas station that has been renamed "The People's Way." I do not make it to all of the meetings, but I do go on a fairly regular basis and consider myself part of the community. We discuss the status of the "24 Demands," mutual aid needs, and many other topics.

At these meetings, we first listen to Black women who are descendants of slaves and Indigenous women. We believe that Black liberation is for the liberation of everyone.

One of the things that I love most about the community is that they care enough to confront me and other people when I or others do or say harmful things.

We believe that community is an antidote to racism.

Having the space and time for people to come together and talk has been a really good thing. It has helped me root some of the white supremacy out of myself.

Many false narratives about George Floyd Square suggest that this location has been harmful to the community. Nothing could be farther from the truth. One false rumor spread about how emergency vehicles were unable to get through. In reality, community members have aided in getting vehicles where they need to go more quickly. We believe that community brings safety. It only makes sense to me that having more people present and watching out for their neighbors is a good thing.

Those who are part of George Floyd Square also support numerous efforts to tend to the material needs of people, including winter gear drives, giveaways, and so many shared meals. The People's Closet where people leave and take clothes and the lending library for books and toys have now been in place for years. The healthcare nonprofit 612 MASH (Minneapolis All Shall Heal), formed from volunteer community members who had helped during the protests, continues to tend to the medical needs of the community, first using a tent and a bus, and now a bricks-and-mortar free primary care clinic.

In the Square, care is taken to support accessibility for people with a wide variety of disabilities. A wheelchair ramp was added near the site of George Floyd's death, seating is made available for people that need it, and American Sign Language interpreters are present for large events. Quiet space is offered for those needing a break, and care is taken when people become emotionally dysregulated. We could always do better.

George Floyd Square has exemplified the elusive "beloved community" more than any church I have witnessed. You may find the beloved community in surprising places too—places where people authentically listen to and care for one another.

CHAPTER 6
TEXTS WITH FRIENDS

When I showed up at Holy Trinity Lutheran Church (HTLC) on Monday, June 1, 2020, I encountered a chaotic scene. In my previous career as a music therapist, I had experience working in inpatient psychiatric units, so I felt comfortable talking with people in acute distress. I sought out the leaders and told them that I was going to work on de-escalation. They thought that sounded good.

People were showing up with carloads, truckloads, even vanloads of food and supplies that were unloaded onto the lawn of the church. Human chains of people passed the supplies from one person to another into the church building for sorting. Sorted supplies were then distributed at tables set up outside. An unmoving, growing crowd of people had gathered in front of these tables. In my estimation, the growing and unmoving crowd was full of people who seemed desperate and had likely been through experiences of scarcity before. Likely some of them were refugees who had fled difficult situations. I imagined that the determined women in the front of the distribution tables who did not move were afraid and attempting to get supplies for their families. Because of the crowd around the tables, many people could not get access.

My go-to action in times of crisis is to reach out to other people. I know that things go much better when I work together with others. In 2021, I started more intensive personal work with Rozella Haydée White as my spiritual life coach. One of the important things I learned from Rozella is the importance and value of being "grounded and surrounded." This involves being clear about my values, moving with intention, and being connected with other people.

A key thing I have learned from my journey of rooting white supremacy out of myself is the importance of not assuming that I have all of the answers to problems that I don't fully understand. It is important to ask questions and more important to *listen*. It is especially important to listen to people who are the most affected by any given situation. Charging ahead alone without consultation is not a good idea. After landing in this chaotic scene, I knew that it would be a good idea to reach out to some friends.

When I caught my breath, I started a text thread with Rev. Dr. Jia Starr Brown and Dr. Kelly Sherman-Conroy. Our thread is still active today—I have collaborated with Jia and Kelly on anti-racism work in the church for several years. I needed to be surrounded and grounded by these friends—and I just needed some plain old help. The situation at Holy Trinity was ripe for "white savior complex" to emerge and for harm to be done by white people to folks who were showing up for assistance. People needing assistance were already hurting and traumatized. The last thing they needed was more harm.

Kelly and Jia deeply understand the need for cultural awareness. We helped each other stay in tune with the need to prevent harm that could be caused by people or practices lacking in cultural competence. Our text conversations were a lifeline for me. Both Kelly and Jia have granted permission for me to include some of them here; they may help convey some of the immediacy I felt. Our texts range from responding to immediate material needs of the community to our collective lack of sleep to our concerns about COVID, with times for celebrating moments of joy as well.

Dr. Kelly Sherman-Conroy, whose Lakota name is Mato Wašté Winyan or Good Bear Woman, is a member of the Oglala Lakota Nation. Kelly is the first native woman theologian with a doctorate degree in the ELCA! She has a passion for social justice, racial reparations, healing, and storytelling with more than two decades of experience teaching and leading in ministry. Kelly has organized "movement chaplains" and was careful to train them in cultural awareness. These movement chaplains showed up at many places in the Twin Cities, including the distribution site at HTLC. The movement chaplains provided a ministry of presence and were tuned into the need to disrupt harmful practices.

Rev. Dr. Jia Starr Brown is an African American lesbian pastor, educator, and activist in the Twin Cities, with more than two decades of experience advocating for underrepresented communities. With a heart for community and access for all, she stands—and activates—as a truth-teller at the intersection of faith, education, and justice. Jia and I organized several vigils in George Floyd Square and often showed up together for protests, mutual aid, and online trainings and debriefings.

Below are excerpts from our yearslong text thread that began on June 1, 2020. I am very grateful for the presence of these friends during this tender time.

JUNE 1, 2020 11:08 A.M.

Shari: It's wild here—I just got on site and am going to jump into de-escalation.

Jia: What is going on, Shari?? Tell me if I need to be somewhere. Just called you.

Kelly: What's going on? I'm just getting freed up.

Shari: Call me?

Jia: I just did but missed you. In a meeting until noon. Kelly, can you call and then text me details in this chat?

Kelly: Jia, they need help with crowd control at Holy Trinity and getting organized. I'm working on support.

Jia: What kind of support is needed? Is clergy needed or is it riot stuff?

Shari: Not riot.

Shari: Clergy would be helpful.

Shari: Calm presence.

Jia: Okay. I will call in a sec.

Jia: Shari, what are the size of diapers needed?

Shari: Sizes 4-6 are biggest need.

Jia: You want them brought to HTLC?

Shari: Yes.

Kelly: I've got 6 people coming. Two have some crisis experience to be able to control and help better and three have cultural awareness training or experience.

Kelly: Hope that helps.

Jia: Sending out word for diapers now.

Shari: If people have sawhorses or some other barrier that would be helpful.

Kelly: Hmmmm I will think.

Shari: Not necessary but would be nice.

Jia: Hmm.

Jia: Some volunteers are bringing diapers now.

Shari: Great.

Shari: Scarcity vibe here.

Jia: Whew.

Jia: Comfortable with me making a fb [Facebook] post about diapers needed at HTLC?

Jia: I know that will mobilize more folks.

Shari: Yes please / drive and drop in front of church.

Jia: Folks are on the way with diapers. You still need a barricade or something?

Jia: I can try to update my status and add to comments. Or one of you can add to comments if needed.

Kelly: I've not found barricades yet but have people looking.

Shari: Not urgent.

Jia: Okay. Feel free to add additional needs to my fb page.

Jia: Folks want to know what else is needed.

Shari: Laundry soap, dish soap.

Shari: Trash bags.

Jia: LOT OF DIAPERS COMING YOUR WAY. CALM PASTORAL PRESENCE POSSIBLY COMING AS WELL.

Shari: [Thumbs-up emoji]

Jia: Shari, I gave your name to [redacted name]—bringing car loads very soon.

Jia: Okay to give your number to them?

Shari: Yes.

Jia: He ran a diaper drive and is asking if wipes are needed.

Shari: Running to the bathroom.

Shari: Yes wipes.

Shari: Charging my phone a bit.

Shari: But he can call—back soon.

Jia: Sorry, misunderstood his message. Didn't ask about wipes. Said he has access to a business that acts as a diaper bank.

Jia: HE IS ALSO TRAINED IN DE-ESCALATION.

Jia: SO THIS WILL BE GREAT.

Jia: Connecting you two on fb.

Kelly: There is a van coming with baby stuff you need. They said it's a white van. And trash bags.

Kelly: [Redacted] in orange is a crisis trauma pastor. He can help. I told him to find you. Super nice guy.

Jia: [Redacted] is 5 min. away Shari.

Jia: Connected you two on fb.

Shari: Jia—have him approach from the east going west.

Shari: I'll go out front now.

Kelly: I'm headed out soon to the Protest at Governor's Residence. Please be safe. If you need more people let me know and I can send some more I think. Just text cuz I'm not checking email much right now.

Kelly: Be safe. [purple heart emoji]

Jia: LMK when [redacted] makes it.

Jia: Just want to make sure y'all connect.

Shari: Connected with [redacted].

Jia: Great thanks.

JUNE 2, 2020, 11:16AM

Kelly: Hey! How are you doing today, Shari? Any needs?

Jia: Here's what she shared with me.

Jia: Cooking oil, diapers still, personal hygiene stuff.

Kelly: Okay. Any special size?

Jia: She said that smaller sizes are better than larger.

Jia: Will go farther.

Kelly: Got it.

Kelly: Sending you both love today.

Shari: Hi. Hot items for HTLC—cooking oil, dish soap, laundry soap, body wash, paper products. Really the hottest thing is oil. As Jia said, smaller containers of things are helpful as many people are on foot so it's harder to carry the big containers and also [our] supplies last longer. I am going to check with [redacted] for updates and can pass that on.

Shari: When I left, diapers were okay, but it is kind of a constant need. Sizes 4-6 were requested the most.

Shari: Okay, just talked with someone at HTLC—they are now updating things on their Facebook page—so that is the most current information. Some current urgent needs—water, Gatorade, coolers of ice, tuna, etc. Check out the page for a full list.

Shari: Kelly, the setup is WAY BETTER today. People are getting numbers and are waiting in lines and then more people are able to get what they need. I'm hopeful that it will be more calm and just humane.

Shari: Please amplify the HTLC posts.

Kelly: Hey that's great! I've heard it seems to be going better. Today is difficult to get help but I have some for later the other days. The March is taking everyone right now lol.

Shari: I'm on communications if y'all need anything amplified or anything.

Kelly: I have four carloads of water that was to go to the Saint Paul march but cannot get a hold of anyone. Ugh. I will work it out.

Shari: You could take it to HTLC.

JUNE 2, 2020, 4:26PM

Shari: OMG—Jen Collins is going to the hospital to "prepare to meet my baby girl."

Kelly: She's early!

Shari: Oh boy, I hope not too early.

Kelly: Keep me posted on any needs you hear!

Shari: Kelly, I am still working on finding you a place to get away. Stay tuned.

Kelly: Awww thanks. I broke down in my staff meeting yesterday. Wasn't the place, I will tell you that.

Shari: I'm so sorry.

Shari: I just got a call from my company RE/MAX Results. They see what I am doing and want to know how they can help.

Jia: Heading up to Holy Trinity with 2 plus kids around 12:30.

Jia: Older kids who can help.

Shari: [Thumbs-up emoji]

Kelly: I will be by there with lots of water.

Kelly: Chaplains stepped up their presence so you should see more.

Shari: Kelly, it's people with the complexion of colonialism who are clueless.

Shari: Jia, LMK when you think you are going to go. I want to check in there. I THINK things are kind of stabilized and HTLC has their systems set up now. I am thinking I can pull back from there and focus on other things.

Kelly: I've had good reports from there this a.m. Much organized.

Shari: [Thumbs up emoji]

Jia: Hey. In a meeting for another hour, then planned to go get kids. Angela asked for POC to be present and visible to lend a hand. Is that not needed anymore?

Jia: So glad to hear that things are going well.

Kelly: I think it's needed.

Kelly: I have to get this church garden planted. They delivered the soil and just dumped it! But I can be by later.

Shari: Yes, I think it is needed too. I'm going to check in with folks when I get there.

Shari: I'm being pulled into stuff happening at Calvary.

JUNE 3, 2020, 12:29PM

Shari: Jia, how's it going? I want to jump in the shower before I go over to HTLC.

Jia: I am just now leaving the meeting. Heading home to eat, see kids, and then we can head out. I'm sorry, I know help is needed. Doing my best.

Kelly: I've had 5 more show up.

Kelly: I'm still planting.

Jia: Leaving here in 15.

Kelly: Jia, I took your advice and tried melatonin last night. May have taken too much or too early and I was out super early. But I slept. [heart]

Shari: I'm so glad!

Jia: I'm so glad you slept. I know you needed it. We all need rest. And water!

Shari: Jia, I hope you are not planning on going to the memorial service today.

Jia: Why?

Shari: It seems so risky to be inside with COVID.

Shari: [anxious face emoji]

Jia: Hmm . . . .

Shari: What do you think about it?

Jia: Idk. I was invited and offered tickets.

Shari: Like I can't imagine there won't be singing.

Shari: I imagine social distancing will be extremely difficult—it's bad enough outside.

Kelly: I think it's a difficult decision but there is a solid concern of COVID. It's an enclosed space and most likely no social distancing. If you do go, perhaps do what they are asking and quarantine after and get tested?

Shari: I can definitely understand you wanting to go and maybe feeling like you should go, but . . . I really wish they would have picked an outside venue.

Jia: They are doing fever tests I think.

Shari: I think I am going to get tested.

Jia: I need to think about it.

Shari: Fever tests don't really do anything—people are contagious and asymptomatic for 14 days before they get sick.

Kelly: [Pastes in screen shot from state of MN] We recommend that any Minnesotan who has attended a protest, vigil, or community clean-up get tested for #COVID19. If you start to feel sick, get tested right away. If you do not feel sick, get tested as soon as you can, but no later than 5-7 days after the event.

Kelly: This was sent to me by the bishop for me to remind all the chaplains volunteering.

Shari: Yeah I'm actually kind of worried about it for myself—mainly because James is SOOOOO anxious about COVID—it would not go well if I got sick. I'm going to try to be more careful about distancing, which is extremely difficult for me.

Jia: Going to talk with Jennifer about it now. I'll circle back.

Shari: I'm going to watch from home.

Jia: We are not going to go.

Jia: Will watch online.

Kelly: This brings up a good point. How do you help people with the struggle of wanting to help or be present physically but are nervous because we are still in the midst of the pandemic?

Jia: Right. That's really what all this is about.

Jia: And I hate this. Bc I want to go bear witness.

JUNE 4, 2020, 12:09 P.M.

Shari: I am going to watch on TV. Kelly, I have to think it will be on MPR—so you could listen on your drive.

Shari: Calvary has been dealing with the need to make some radical change because we can't really afford our building. We've had a deficit budget for years, etc. So we've been having all of these listening sessions. Now some folks are saying "I know—let's save the brown and black people" "Let's make our church a center for them." I'm saying "and let's not be white saviors. White folks are the broken ones. Nothing is going to change until white folks start digging into rooting white supremacy out of ourselves and our institutions."

Kelly: Have you asked or talked with BIPOC in your area or organizations about what they think of that idea?

Jia: I completely agree with Kelly—people should be included in the decisions that involve them. Wondering about planning a convo with BIPOC community members, orgs to invite their perspective.

Shari: I totally agree—we need to talk with neighbors. Trying to think about how to do that without centering Calvary.

Jia: Maybe have someone else guide the conversation.

Jia: There are some cool ways to do that.

Jia: Someone who cares about Calvary and the community.

Shari: Hmmmm.

Kelly: Well, at the moment Calvary is the center because you have to figure out what to do. So don't get too ashamed just yet. And I agree with Jia. Have someone guide it for you. Step outside your circle you've been using at Calvary. Someone invested in the community.

Jia: Like, (for example), I have led community conversations on behalf of a congregation or effort before. I used to do that for the county a long time ago.

Jia: Yes yes.

Shari: I am thinking of our next-door neighbor who was involved in starting MPD 150 [a 150-year review of the Minneapolis Police Department].

Jia: To talk directly to the people.

Kelly: See . . . You can do it. When you start putting up barriers, just take a step back and reassess a bit. Look at the vision in a new way.

Shari: Okay, I was having a block about this—this is helpful.

Jia: You can do it!

◆ ◆ ◆

NOVEMBER 3, 2020, 9:38 A.M.—ELECTION DAY

Shari: We got this!! How are y'all this morning?

Kelly: Been up since 3:30.

Kelly: 4th cuppa tea and two sodas down.

Shari: Trouble sleeping or too much to do?

Kelly: Too much to do.

Kelly: Just finished delivering coffee and politely arguing with a Trump supporter.

Shari: Where?

Kelly: MLK Park off Nicollet.

Shari: Wow, that is a little surprising.

Kelly: They were voting and we were handing out coffee and talking. She was just bitchy.

Kelly: How are you?

Shari: Good – lots of connecting with folks about community presence and rapid response @ Calvary. I needed to make a family breakfast for the sake of family sanity. Heading to Calvary soon. Pastor Hans and I have first shift.

Kelly: Hang in there.

Jia: Hey y'all. Good morning. Been going for the past couple weeks at 100 mph with work and community stuff. Fragility abounds. Everywhere. I am tired and empty. Was planning on getting out for a couple hours, but woke up and sensed that I needed to be home. Kids are scared about the election, and my future son-in-law is on the ballot here in AV for City Council. I gotta take off my pastor hat for at least part of the day and just be a mom. And a scared black woman.

Jia: Thanks for all you two are doing today. Grateful for you.

DECEMBER 4, 2020 8:58 P.M.

Shari: Something's up at the square—I'm heading over. We're 12 squad cars in—someone arrested.

Kelly: Oh no.

Jia: Yeah, been in touch with a few Folx—waiting to hear if I need to drive over.

Kelly: Keep me posted.

Jia: Since you're heading over, can you let me know what you see when you get there?

Jia: This is nuts. I'm so tired of us being tired.

Kelly: What happened?

Jia: Waiting to hear—I'm in like 3 different chats about it.

Shari: Okay for tonight. Talking to Marcia.

Kelly: Ok. I'm headed back from Shakopee. Keep me posted.

Jia: Just got a call for black folx to gather at the square. There in 15.

Jia: Going to stop by and see if support is needed, just a presence.

Kelly: Be safe. [praying hands]

Shari: I walked Jia and Jennifer down to the square. I left a bit ago. Jia was still talking with folks. I plan to go to the meeting at 8:00 a.m. Things did seem calm for the time being—more dynamics going on than I am aware of.

DECEMBER 5, 2020, 7:28 A.M.

Kelly: I'm glad things calmed.

DECEMBER 5, 2020, 9:42 A.M.

Jia: Hey y'all, good morning. I didn't get home until almost 12—didn't want to text that late. Things are calm, folks are triggered and angry. Discussing next steps and ways to respond if/when that happens again.

Jia: Thanks for sending out the word yesterday, Shari. Really appreciate the chain of communication.

Shari: Thanks for the update Jia. Update for you is that there will be a new Signal group created just for calling people to the square in acute situations.

Shari: Jia, do you want me to add you to the Calvary rapid response thread? Kelly is on that thread. Totally up to you—you are probably looped in enough with other threads.

◆ ◆ ◆

MAY 4, 2021, 6:00 P.M.

This was the day of an online interfaith gathering organized by Jia that was held after the verdict for Derek Chauvin was announced.

Shari: Just text me if there are any notes you want me to hit.

Jia: [Purple heart emoji]

Jia: This session may be hard for some folks.

Shari: K.

Shari: White folks?

Kelly: Yup.

Jia: Yep. Glad you're here.

Kelly: You on Shari?

Shair: Yep.

Kelly: Woot.

Shari: Please nudge me if needed.

Jia: One of us will text you if so.

Shari: [Thumbs up emoji]

MAY 4, 2021, 7:31 P.M.

Jia: Whew. Idk what folks are thinking . . . lol! How did the small group go?

Shari: I know I wish I could hear what people are thinking.

Shari: My group was okay—all older white women.

Jia: Stoic expressions . . .

MAY 11, 2021, 2:28 P.M.

Shari: Hey thinking of you two tonight. I have an EDLARJ board meeting 6:00-7:30 tonight.

Jia: The White Board!

Shari: [Laughter and tears emoji]

Kelly: White People Whisperer support group.

Jia: Shari does anything BUT whisper!!

Shari: Welp – I am officially the president of the White Board!

CHAPTER 7
WEEKS, MONTHS, YEARS AFTER

It is a joy to continue to journey together way beyond the initial march and early days. The community that continues to gather at George Floyd Square for justice and Black liberation is nothing short of a miracle. This active protest has lasted longer than the Montgomery Bus Boycott in Alabama, 1955–56. Truly, the community at George Floyd Square has shown me what "beloved community" looks like.

Calvary Lutheran Church's proximity to the site of the tragic murder of George Floyd and the readiness of enough Calvary people allowed us to be church in ways that church was always meant to be. We tried to follow what Jesus taught in word and deed by being with marginalized people, giving up power, and confronting empire. We set down notions of respectability and white saviorism and *listened* to the needs and cares of others. We continue to live into what Martin Luther regarded as most important—care of the neighbor. I have boundless gratitude for the opportunity to be a part of both the community at George Floyd Square and the Calvary community. The boundaries are permeable between the two communities, and to some degree, they have blessed one another.

As I mentioned in chapter 5, Calvary's Community Table and the south barricade were across the street from each other—we shared an intersection. Check-ins between people at the table and the barricade happened naturally because of our close proximity. As relationships developed, conversations got deeper and ideas about collaboration expanded. In the beginning there were a number of people who acted as community security at the Square and other places in Minneapolis and Saint Paul. (We certainly couldn't rely on the police.)

At one point, because of security concerns, people proposed the idea of using Calvary's bell tower for security surveillance. After discussions about safety, Calvary leaders agreed to allow two people at a time into the bell tower.

When there seemed to be a credible threat against Calvary, security from George Floyd Square offered to watch Calvary as well. After more conversation, Calvary leadership installed a security camera that covered the intersection of 39th Street and Chicago Avenue and made the video available when requested.

Calvary Lutheran Church is a small congregation without a lot of financial resources, but we were able to fill some material needs. On several occasions, tables, chairs, tents, and stage pieces were needed for events happening in George Floyd Square that were led by a wide variety of efforts and organizations. Calvary's small staff could not meet all of the incoming requests, so members stepped in to help fill those needs. Honestly, sometimes it got a little tiring transporting all of these supplies outside and then back into the building. But we knew it was important and were honored to do it.

On one night, events ran late and I was too weary to stay out late enough to return everything, so I left three stage pieces outside. Those stage pieces had been used by George Floyd's family members and the Reverend Jesse Jackson to address the crowd that night. Those three pieces remain in the Square now and continue to be used as needed.

Amazingly, Calvary allowed use of one of our kitchens! (As I understand it, kitchens are one of the places where churches are least likely to relinquish control.) A small group of community members was dedicated to ongoing feeding of people in the neighborhood. Some of the cooks were working out of tiny apartments, while others lived several miles away. It just made sense to use Calvary's kitchen because of its size and proximity to the Square. For several months, the cooks using Calvary's kitchen fed many people.

Some aid—like tables, chairs, stage pieces, and kitchen use—was given as the result of requests. Other aid—like preparing to offer sanctuary space and providing materials for prayer flags—was given as a result of discernment. People were encouraged to "bring their gifts" to the Square. This call helped put myself and others in a posture of discernment about what we could bring.

When Jacob Blake was shot and seriously injured by Rusten Sheskey, a police officer in Kenosha, Wisconsin, on August 23, 2020, the George Floyd Square community members felt deeply disturbed. Some people traveled to Kenosha to join and support the protest there, and conversation began about having a vigil at George Floyd Square. After sitting with it for a bit, I offered to put together a multifaith vigil for Jacob Blake at George Floyd Square. Through my relationships with MARCH (Multifaith Anti-Racism, Change, & Healing), I knew I could quickly pull together a group of multifaith clergy and faith leaders to help lead a vigil. I reached out to my friend Rev. Dr. Jia Starr Brown to help organize the vigil. I love organizing and thinking through things with Jia! An amazing group of leaders came together to lead the vigil that night.

During this time, my racial justice journey involved "just showing up and listening." My go-to posture was to not take the mic, but to pass the mic to Black and brown people and to be quiet. Jia encouraged me to speak at this vigil. "I think you have something to say," she told me. I thought and prayed carefully about whether I should speak and what would be important for me to say as a white-bodied Lutheran woman in this context and moment. I decided that the thing that I should do was to renounce evil and ask the crowd to renounce evil with me. This is what I said:

> My name is Shari Seifert, and I follow a brown-skinned Palestinian Jewish man who flipped tables and was executed by the state for standing up for his friends. I follow this man named Jesus and am Christian and specifically Lutheran from Calvary Lutheran Church.
>
> Good white Christians, I am so glad that you are here—but we need to talk! I need to know—and I need you to think about—if you are also a follower of this man named Jesus. What do pictures of Jesus look like in your church? Does your church equate white and lightness with "good" and dark and blackness with "bad" or "evil"? Are you unwittingly a part of the church of white supremacy? Friends who are part of other faith traditions or no faith tradition—do you unknowingly hold up white supremacy? I don't mean to shock you, but I don't have time to play. People are dying.
>
> Still.
>
> We can't do this anymore.
>
> The Sunday after George Floyd was killed was Pentecost on our church calendar. Today is the thirteenth Sunday after Pentecost. We're still counting Sundays in this Pentecost season, and the fires are still burning, and the Spirit is still moving, and we can't have churches of respectability that center whiteness any more.
>
> We have to stop.
>
> George Floyd Square is where we hold fast and say "no more." We're not doing that anymore. We have to proclaim that #Black Lives Matter. Like Rev. [and author] Lenny Duncan said, the task of the twentieth-century church is dismantling white supremacy. We need to get busy! We need to renounce the evil—the heresy—of white supremacy.

I guided people through renouncing evil as we faced the four directions.

Face the north. Do you renounce the evil of equating whiteness with "good" and black and darkness with "bad"? If so, answer "We renounce it!"

Face the east. Do you renounce the evil of racial profiling, sentences that are too harsh for Black folks, and extrajudicial killing of Black people by police? If so, answer "We renounce it!"

Face the south. Do you renounce the evil of too-lenient sentences for white men who kill Black folks, who are rewarded with trips to Burger King and obscenely large GoFundMe accounts? If so, answer "We renounce it!"

Face the west. Do you renounce the evil of white supremacy? If so, answer "We renounce it!"

Speaking these words with the crowd at George Floyd Square felt deeply right. I was grateful that Jia had encouraged me to speak, that Calvary members were there at the vigil, and that Pastor Hans livestreamed it. Jia and I would go on to organize a few more vigils for the Square.

Soon after the vigil for Jacob Blake, I learned that Marcia Howard, my son's former high school teacher and George Floyd Square regular, had slept through the night after that first vigil. It was the first time she had done so since George Floyd was murdered. This was a time of 24/7 security in the Square, so Marcia sleeping through the night was quite an accomplishment! I was very happy to hear the news, and it made me think that Calvary was showing up as an anchor for the community in a good way so that people could get a little rest.

◆ ◆ ◆

It has been an intense time since the city lynched a man a block from my church. (My use of the word "lynching" throughout this book is intentional. Lynchings are public executions without trial. They are meant to elicit terror and to control the populace.) Thinking through all of the events and the trauma while writing this book has been difficult *and* healing for me. As I write, we are still engaged in an active and ongoing protest at the Square. However, I haven't engaged in a lot of in-depth conversations with George Floyd Square community members about the early days. I wanted to check some of my memories and hear the perspectives from four longtime neighbors who became active in George Floyd Square: Katie Dillon, Susan Hinemann, Marcia Howard, and Jenny Jones. They took time for conversation with me one evening about the intersection of Calvary Lutheran Church and George Floyd Square and helped me gain a better understanding of the impact of the vigils on community members.

Jenny Jones shared this:

It's hard to necessarily distinguish between Calvary and Shari. One of the things that was really meaningful to me, as a little bit more of an outsider, was the first vigil. It was raining, and there were all the different groups. That was so amazing, and so beautiful, and that you would act as a convener of all these different faiths and use your proximity to the Square to orchestrate that was so meaningful. It gave so many people in the city a different perspective on the Square. I feel like they had an excuse to come that they didn't have before, and they saw the meaning of it and the sacredness of it.

Marcia Howard shared this:

That part. You know, at the very beginning, when we first started meeting, we talked about, and I think they were community member Julia Eagles's words: **we wanted to keep that place secure, we wanted to keep it sustainable, and we wanted to keep it sacred.** And the consecration of George Floyd Square as a place of mourning and a place of prayer for interfaith pilgrims that came to that space—it was even for those of us that are irreligious. It was so, so important to see multidenominations, multifaith folks being convened in that one moment, because the entire world stood up for this protest, and the coordination of having all those people there and then the fact that it was almost like a tradition. We've had multiple vigils. And so if there's this idea that, given time, the sacredness of the space will peter away and then they would go back to business as usual, or status quo, trust and believe the powers that be, hope that that is and so want that to be so, and yet, year after year—we are going on our third year—year after year, people still come. Not only do pastors still come, faith groups still come, but even the families who've participated in those vigils still come. In fact, Emmet Till's family would go to Say Their Names Cemetery. And we echo the same process of the vigil, whether it's Butchy with his trumpet or our Pastor Jia saying a word, people know that there is a sacredness to this space, that it is no small thing. It is no flash-in-the-pan of protest, significance, and then nothing else. I think that that is going to, whether all of us were to move away, George Floyd Square, I think, will still hold some of that, because it's been set.

There were many times when we feared that the city would create a violent confrontation in the Square, particularly when we suspected that the city was going to remove the barricades and open up the streets that first year of the uprising. Plans were made to help keep people safe. A small group at Calvary met and discussed how we could help. Calvary had recently acted as a "sanctuary supporting" congregation for an immigrant family, meaning we were part of a support network for people who were seeking sanctuary inside of another house of faith. It made sense for us to offer sanctuary to people who may be harmed by police or white supremacist action.

We consulted with people from Holy Trinity Lutheran Church who had provided refuge for protesters and housed medics while the Third Precinct burned. They had not had the benefit of planning in advance! They helped us think through some things and provided helpful information about planning for lapses in electricity, writing a communication plan, and developing logistics for treating people who had been teargassed. (They learned the hard way that pouring milk to treat people's teargassed eyes led to carpeted floors that needed replacement.) Their ideas helped us create a good communication strategy.

I reached out to an organized street medic group to work out a plan for them to show up if needed. We learned that it was better for all parties to designate a place for street medics to help people outside of Calvary's property.

We collected snacks, food, walkie-talkies, nozzled water bottles for washing out eye irritants, milk for washing out eye irritants, spare clothes, and kiddie pools for people to stand in while they got their eyes washed out.

In consultation with George Floyd Square community members, we made so many plans for how our sanctuary and rapid response efforts would work:

> social distancing
> stations where people could charge their phones
> tracking who came in
> keeping guns out of the building
> designating where chaplains could meet with people
> designating where people could sit quietly by themselves
> requiring police to show search warrants through specific windows before letting them enter the building
> what rooms we would use
> what rooms we would close off
> routes cars could take to move people from Calvary as needed
> how many people we would need at a time to staff these efforts

I kept a "go bag" packed and in my car in case I needed to be at the church overnight or for a few days.

We had a five-member core team that was empowered to make quick decisions and a larger team to respond as needed. We sought the approval from the executive team of Calvary's church council. It is no small thing that they said yes. I believe Pastor Hans was working in the background to help get to this yes.

We made all of these plans—and never ended up needing to use Calvary as a place of refuge. That is a good thing. We occasionally would bring ourselves back to a higher state of readiness based on what was happening in the community, including reconnecting with street medics. I learned that all of that planning mattered to the community.

We could have easily thought of all of our planning as a waste. But after this eye-opening conversation with our four long term neighborhood residents about the significance of our "rapid response" plans, I was glad that we planned as we did.

Here are some excerpts from that conversation.

Marcia Howard:

As the first year of the protest went on, leadership at Calvary became increasingly involved in community conversations about what community looks like and what safety looks like. I definitely felt as if Calvary was in a position of "What can we do to help? What can we do to help within limits of what we could do as a church?"

If we were to be attacked, where would we, like in *The Hunchback of Notre Dame*, be able to knock on the door and say, "Sanctuary"? If we cried "Sanctuary," who would afford us that? We had people in the neighborhood during the conflict, several neighbors, who allowed us to come into their homes. Thank you, Susan. Thank you, Kate. But then we had another neighbor, which was Calvary, who at a certain point said, "We will provide refuge as well," and for that I will be eternally grateful.

Susan Hineman:

I just want to underscore that, too, with thinking of how many churches and synagogues have provided sanctuary spaces for immigrants. But in this very, very planful way, where these discussions and preparations, and setting up, and all of this, all of this planning, and to be a sanctuary for your neighbors, like immediately, I mean I've seen religious institutions do that if there's an actual disaster, but to do it for a political disaster, you know, and under political threat, Calvary's not just willingness, but ability to turn it around really, really quick was pretty amazing.

Jenny Jones:

I feel like it went beyond just opening your doors and being there—any request we have had, it seemed to me you were so generous with, you know, loaning the kitchen or loaning the stage, or just anything we asked. The ask was at the very least respected, if not fulfilled.

Marcia Howard:

I think at a certain point that it was even beyond asking, when members of the congregation and church leadership started coming to community meetings. **I made that analogy of we're in this boat, and we all need to start to row and put our back into it. They were sitting beside us in the boat, and so we say, bring your gifts to the Square.**

They had a lot of gifts that they were willing to bring to the Square that we didn't have to ask for. There were needs that were met that we didn't have to ask for.

So even that the idea that after the first year that summer that we would be set upon by the city of Minneapolis, this plan for creating sanctuary at Calvary Lutheran was a coordinated thing. It wasn't as if the idea was that if the guests and community members in George Floyd Square were to have been set upon, they would just run to the church, and that was it.

That took time and coordination, it took supplies, and I can go into that more, but y'all, we were on my porch. We were at Calvary. This was planful and it was thoughtful. They were saying that if the City of Minneapolis were to set upon us, they were providing us a place to triage. We had kiddie pools, we had milk to pour over us. We had charging stations and snacks. They're coordinating a team of drivers to take us out from the building in the dead of night to our locations. East, west, north, south. It was a huge plan.

It was so huge, in fact, that it could not have been just one neighborhood member's vanity project, that wasn't just an idea of just Shari in order to just stay with the people at the fire, because that involved all of their congregants. It involved their insurance. It involved the risk to their church, because remember, we had hundreds of people in that Square on a regular basis, and so to coordinate the evacuation of all those people as they head south down Chicago Avenue into a building. . . .

Had it ever been truly necessary, it would have been written about in history books—the plan for it should be written about in history books.

It should be written about in pamphlets. It should be written about in college instruction.

It should be written about, because that is what it meant to be community for that church—their security cameras that they put in place for us, that they gave us access to when axe-wielding idiots showed up.

We have been under siege. My shift was 3 o'clock, and y'all, I live about forty steps from the west barricade, and I felt somehow safer being on the end of Chicago Avenue, because I had that bell tower sort of watching over me. There's no religiosity in it. It's this idea that between Calvary and Keith's surveillance, I had somebody watching me at 3 in the morning.

And I also had comrades on that block. I knew I could jump out of that guard shack and run to Cavalry or run to Arash's, or run to Katie's house, or run to Madi's house.

That's why we [the community in George Floyd Square] ain't been rolled [by police or others]. They could not, they could not, they could not. When all of

Chicago Avenue, when they wanted to turn everybody on that stretch of road against us, and it was hard, and I know for you, Katie, who actually lived there, you've talked to your neighbors.

But I'm telling you the reason the city could not win is because where there's people, there's power. And it was too many of us, even people that they thought would have been predisposed to be against us. Well-heeled congregants of a Lutheran church that's one hundred years old. "Oh, there's no way they could possibly be with the rebels." And yet time and time again, Calvary stood up for us on our side.

Katie Dillon:

Not to be glib about it, but if anybody would say that, my answer is "Clearly you've not heard of this guy called Jesus."

Marcia Howard:

I'm just sort of like, the Lutheran church is Calvary to me. Having this particular congregation having to make a stand, I was incredibly touched. I was touched. I've been touched, and I know it seems like I'm waxing poetic about it, but it's no small thing.

It's no small thing. It's no small thing that they walked what other people talk, and they would have had to suffer the consequences of it.

Someone at Calvary had the idea of putting up a banner for George Floyd on the church. That idea was quickly put together with the artwork that Ella Endo had done with the words that George Floyd's loved ones had used to describe him. (Chapter 9 details how it took a lot of discussion and time for Calvary to put up a Black Lives Matter banner. The path for putting up a banner for George Floyd was made easier in part because Pastor Hans was working in the background.)

Calvary's Race Equity Committee worked with Ella on banner design. Ella wanted it to be big enough so that people could read the words used to describe George Floyd. I think many were stunned by the commanding presence of the banner. It definitely had an effect on the neighborhood. It was a signal to many that Calvary was in the fight for justice and was with the community. After the banner was up for a few months, I learned from Angela Harrelson, George Floyd's aunt, that she really loved and appreciated the banner. Ella eventually gave many of George Floyd's family members some of the T-shirts that she created using the same image.

Neighbor Katie Dillon shared her thoughts about the banner this way: "Calvary really was showing up and walking the walk. There was the banner.

Clearly, it was shown, you know, that you all had done a lot of work, and were really ready to be present."

For many years Calvary struggled with a deficit budget, with a building that needed repair and was beyond what our small congregation needed. Dedicated members spent years trying to find a solution for our situation. We explored sharing our building with other congregations or moving in with another congregation. Nothing ever quite worked out. We didn't want to leave our corner. We started thinking about selling part of our property to a housing developer. We thought that perhaps we could sell our parking lot or part of our building.

We went into the process with the idea that we would not just sell to the highest bidder, but that we would consider our neighbors and do what is right and helpful for them. Eventually we hired a consultant to accompany and guide us through the process and we got introduced to Trellis, a nonprofit developer of affordable housing. We had an initial plan of selling our parking lot and the education wing to Trellis. When they gave us the price for those parts of our property, the numbers just didn't work.

An idea emerged to have Trellis purchase our whole property and for Calvary to move back in as tenants and to use the renovated former sanctuary rent free. In addition to that, Trellis would provide renovated space for our food shelf. We would be able to stay on the corner of 39th Street and Chicago Avenue, with some time out for renovations. Our building would be turned into deeply affordable housing, and additional deeply affordable housing would be built in the parking lot. It all felt like a miracle. The vote to take this path was a unanimous yes.

One of the 24 Demands is about affordable housing, and it was great that Calvary was able to help meet that demand. I suspect that affordable housing being one of the 24 Demands helped in getting the complicated funding approved by various governmental entities. Everyone was ready for a "win."

These four neighbors shared their views about Trellis developing affordable housing at Calvary.

Susan Hineman:

The barricades were still up when you had the first community meeting about Trellis and the creation of the housing, and I went to it. That was another turning point for me, because it was the first time that I heard a whole bunch of your congregants speak, and I'm suspicious of anyone who has the word "developer" attached to themselves. Folks from the congregation asked every single one of my questions and clearly had thought about it. It was the first time I was really seeing Cavalry other than just kind of taking your and Pastor Hans's word for it, for who the whole community was, and I really appreciated that. I didn't know if you were an outlier, you know, and that proved to me that you really, really weren't.

Jenny Jones:

And there's something so powerful about the larger move that Calvary is making in addressing one of the 24 Demands.

Marcia Howard:

And so the prospect of people from the 4 Corners neighborhood getting an opportunity to be in an affordable home, because the very beginning of that ask had been from a gentleman who was a Denizen of 38, who said "Man, I just want to be able to afford to live in my own neighborhood." That was the beginning of that demand about affordable housing.

Katie Dillon:

You know, a lot of the things that we talk about are the demands and a lot of the things that came out of my own processing of the uprising is when it comes down to it, when you're talking about justice issues, meeting basic needs is a huge part of it. . . . I very much think that that's Calvary showing up in a way that's walking the walk, and is truly, literally, here for the neighborhood in a way that not many other congregations are doing.

Calvary was also privileged to serve as a rehearsal spot and "green room" for performances for the 2021 and 2022 commemorations of George Floyd's death, events called "Rise and Remember." We were honored to host George Floyd's family members, community performers, the artist Common, Sounds of Blackness, the Minnesota Chorale, and others. I was able to hear the most amazing music during this process! One memory that sticks with me is walking George Floyd family members from Calvary to the stage for the concert. We went through an alley, stopped at Marcia Howard's backyard for the right moment, and then headed backstage to wait for their performances and to take in the concert. I was holding the hand of Aunt Laura Stevens all along the way. Aunt Laura had sung "We Shall Overcome" and Aunt Angela Harrelson spoke about having hope for change. Witnessing and having these experiences help to cement my commitment to continue to strive for justice. When you walk with the family like that, you don't go back.

Calvary has been blessed to have Jeanelle Austin, a neighbor and executive director for George Floyd Global Memorial, preach a few times, including for our last service in our building before moving to San Pablo's (Calvary's mother church) while construction was happening. Community member Marcia Howard also spoke at this service, several community members showed up, and community band Brass Solidarity led much of the music.

I preached on the second Pentecost Sunday after George Floyd's lynching along with community members Marcia Howard and Madi R.T. Community member Frank Yellow did the land acknowledgment and Andy Hartin and Everett Ayoubzadeh from the Minneapolis Bahá'í Center of Minneapolis shared music. It has always been a rich time when people from Calvary and George Floyd Square have come together for worship or services in any way.

I expect the relationship between the George Floyd Square community and the Calvary communities to continue for years to come, as we partner to help bring about justice and collective liberation. I look forward to the time when Calvary will be back in and around the building at 39th and Chicago—closer to our neighbors at the Square.

CHAPTER 8
NOT TO EARN ANTI-RACIST PATCHES

Collective liberation is the goal, not earning a bunch of anti-racism patches or learning the right terms to use. The goal should be to root white supremacy out of ourselves. All too often I thought that I should help less fortunate people—that I had a responsibility to bring my ideas to tough situations. What I learned is that people are the best experts on their own lives. I am not here to "save" them. The best thing I can do is to get my boot off of someone else's neck. The best thing I can do is to root white supremacy out of myself.

In the ELCA we begin our services with confession, so I will start the story of my racial justice journey with my own confession.

I am a recovering racist and white supremacist.

I never *chose* to be racist or to embody white supremacist characteristics. I didn't have to—it's part of the programming, part of the systems, part of my inheritance.

I grew up in a very racist country and chances are that you did too. Several years ago, Jonathan Odell, author of *The Healing* and other books dealing with race, visited Calvary Lutheran Church and shared about his experiences of being a recovering racist who grew up in Mississippi. I remember him talking about going from noticing the Black people in iconic photos from the 1960s to noticing the white people. It wasn't a pretty picture. He encouraged us to learn about our history and the places that helped form us, with this process including a review of old newspapers.

FEELING COMFORTABLE EVERYWHERE I WENT

I grew up outside of a Texas town that was so small we didn't even have a local newspaper, so I was left to rely on my memory for this exercise. It took some active work to remember. This process has taken years and is ongoing.

As I understand it, Lexington, Texas, was founded by sixteen families, all involved in the German Methodist church. My dad was heavily involved in this church and loved learning about and keeping the history of the resting place for Lexington's founders. He told me that we had family members who fought on both sides of the Civil War. When I visited the cemetery with an eye towards interrogating my family racial history, I noticed the letters "CSA" on some of my family members' tombstones. When I realized that CSA stands for Confederate States of America, my heart sank a little.

I often heard the story about chains being put on the doors to keep people out of the German Methodist church in Lexington during World War II. My dad said, "It was just a bunch of old men speaking German at the church." At the same time, speaking German in the public schools was discouraged. In the Lexington schools there was a distinction between "the English" and "the Germans." My dad abandoned speaking German and spoke only English. I didn't have the language for it then, but now I recognize that cultural heritage was being traded for taking up the mantle of "whiteness."

After the German Methodist church shut down, my ancestors left that all-white congregation and went to the local Lutheran church—a Missouri Synod (LCMS) congregation that was 100 percent white. This was the church my nuclear family attended as well. We went to church every Sunday and after school on Wednesdays. I remember it being stoic and somber—except when I would get a big bag of candy on Christmas Eve.

My family moved to neighboring Rockdale during my early teen years. I was questioned by a panel of old white men before being confirmed. When I was in high school, my family switched to an American Lutheran Church (ALC) congregation because of the LCMS's stance on women.

I recognize that I grew up with a certain amount of privilege. My dad was the elementary school principal. We lived on a couple hundred acres of land outside of Lexington in a house my parents owned. I usually traveled to and from school with my parents. I felt comfortable everywhere I went.

When my dad's siblings and families would gather, they often shared stories that began with "We were so poor . . ." One story told about my mom going home with my dad for the first time during college and discovering that they had outhouses and no running water in the house. My Granny quit school to help put her brother through law school and my Papa worked in a feed store. They picked cotton, made their own soap, and grew most of their food. This may not sound like a privileged family. But the reality is my family *owned* their own land. This was not a privilege enjoyed by people with darker skin at this time. This land ownership has had ripple effects.

When I was in kindergarten, one day after school I walked the couple blocks to the town square where I was able to walk into the store and buy candy by telling the shopkeeper to put it on my dad's tab. The candy I bought had a racist name, and as far as I knew, no one ever thought anything about it at the time. *Now* I know that having candy with racist names must have been terrible for many folks that didn't look like me—it normalized racist language.

When I was about ten years old I went to Camp Lone Star, an LCMS camp about forty miles from our home. Once again, I felt entirely comfortable entering this space. Some kids from Houston seemed out of their element. When we made a campfire, I amazed some of the city slickers by breaking half-rotten logs on my knee for firewood.

Soon after we arrived at camp, cabin groups came up with their own names for the week. Our counselor's nickname was KK. The name we quickly developed was "KK's Klan." We thought it was funny. We "didn't mean anything by it." We certainly didn't think it was racist.

My memory tells me that there was *one* Black kid at camp from the Houston group. I remember having conversations with "KK's Klan" about dressing up in sheets, going outside, and scaring the boys, because we heard that this kid was going to be camping outside. I don't believe we actually did it. I sure hope not. We thought this was funny. No adults said anything to us about any of it—our cabin name stood the whole week. Now I am horrified by our actions. I wonder what it was like for that one Black kid to be at camp with me while our group joked about KK's Klan. I feel certain that he did not feel entirely comfortable like I did.

If had not been on a journey of learning about my own racism and complicity, I would probably still sincerely think that my actions at Camp Lone Star were just good fun. I am reminded of Maya Angelou's words when she said, "Do the best you can until you know better. Then when you know better, do better." Well, I know better now and am trying to do better.

An important part of learning about the history of where I came from involved talking to and emailing my Texas history teacher Ms. Susie Sansom Piper and her children. I transferred to the schools in Rockdale when I was in sixth grade and benefited from having Ms. Piper as a teacher. Ms. Piper died in 2019 at the age of 98. A few years before her death, she and her children shared with me how she came to teach at the Rockdale school I attended.

Ms. Piper served as the principal of the Aycock School, the school that was "across the tracks" that enrolled Black kids. When school integration happened, the teachers who were Black women were required to have master's degrees and then Black men were required to have doctorate degrees to teach at the newly integrated school.

Ms. Piper was put in charge of "the Black room," a windowless room where the "hopeless kids" were sent. The school administrators wanted Ms. Piper to give up and quit, but giving up was not in her nature! She told me, "It was always my philosophy that everyone counted and everyone could learn." She persevered, and luckily for me she was eventually placed in a mainstream classroom where I benefited from her teaching.

I don't think requiring the Black teachers to have advanced degrees had the desired effect that the architects of exclusion had in mind. It was clear to me that Ms. Piper and Ms. Laura Petty, a Black woman who was my high school biology teacher, were the best teachers in the school. Ms. Piper was a prolific writer and noted historian. She was the keynote speaker at the LBJ Presidential Library on the fiftieth anniversary of the Voting Rights Act of 1965. For many years she wrote a column for the *Rockdale Reporter*, the local newspaper. She was literally writing from her deathbed, including the book *17 Years in the Black Room*, when she died.

It was also clear to me that the children of Ms. Piper and Ms. Petty, fellow students with me, were brilliant. I think I benefited more from school desegregation than the Black kids did. Desegregation brought me better teachers, and I learned that white supremacy is a lie.

I am so mad and sad about the injustice that Ms. Piper went through. I grieve the loss of the gifts and treasures we don't have because other Susie Pipers were put in charge of study hall rather than the classroom. I'm angry about how she and other educators were mistreated. Denying people's gifts and a chance to shine gives us a clear example of how white supremacy and racism harm all of us.

I did not realize these lessons about my childhood and teen years until I circled back around to interrogate my past.

BUILDING SOMETHING NEW

When I graduated from high school and attended Southwest Texas State University, I joined Lutheran Campus Ministry (LCM) and got involved with

Lutheran Student Movement (LSM). Being involved with LCM and LSM brought new meaning to my faith, and it was also where I first experienced multiracial faith spaces, including meeting international students.

For the first time it felt like my faith was connected to the present day and I could be an active participant in it. I *loved* participating in the sessions where resolutions dealing with things like LGBTQ issues and the environment were presented, debated, and voted on at the LSM assemblies. I attended a joint assembly with the Canadian LSM with the theme "Who Is My Neighbor?" One of the assemblies featured a Bible study centered on Micah 6:8: *What does the Lord require of you but to do justice and to love kindness and to walk humbly with your God?* This study was so impactful for me that I can still hear the presenter's voice as he broke down *mishpat, hesed,* and *hashnea.* As is the case for many people of faith involved in justice issues, Micah 6:8 became my *cantus firmus*—the foundational text for my faith.

Working as a peer minister for LCM, I eventually became the regional representative, which covered a couple of states and made me a part of LSM's national council. A memory still with me is a conversation about planning for a future national assembly. Someone put forth the idea of planning an assembly on apartheid in South Africa. Someone wiser than me suggested that instead of an assembly on apartheid in South Africa, we plan an assembly on racism in the United States. Better to work on our own front porch than going into the business of another country.

We chose the topic "Racism in the United States" for the next assembly. Miraculously we were blessed to have C. T. Vivian, civil rights leader and advisor to Rev. Martin Luther King Jr., as the keynote speaker. I can still hear his voice—and the voices of students who argued with him. Student after student stepped up the mic to explain to C. T. Vivian, a man who would go on the be awarded the Presidential Medal of Freedom in 2013 and who Rev. Martin Luther King Jr. described as "the greatest preacher to ever live," that racism didn't exist, or at least did not exist at the LSM national assembly.

During the assemblies, students could step up to the microphone to comment or ask questions. But many of the event's speakers seemed very uncomfortable with conversation around the problems of racism and "fighting" (disagreeing). I remember one white speaker proclaiming "I danced with a Black person last night." I watched C. T. Vivian tell a string of white students to sit down. "Do you know who I am?" he asked. I was pretty nervous when I stepped up to the mic. I knew there was a good chance that I would be told to sit down too, but I had to say something. From my memory of the event,

I said something like this: "I am *glad* that we are fighting, because racism is a problem and we need to talk about it." I paused so that C.T. Vivian could tell me to go sit down. Instead, he told me, "Keep talking." I took C.T. Vivian's charge to keep talking seriously—so I am still talking.

My relationships with people involved in LCM and LSM were grounding for me. When I transferred to Sam Houston State University in Huntsville, Texas, to pursue a degree in music therapy, I discovered that there was no Lutheran Campus Ministry present, so I decided that I needed to start one. I was a student advisor of a joint ALC/LCMS campus ministry board. I talked to someone on the board about my desire to start a new program, and they pitched the idea of giving me a little money to support my efforts. I wasn't looking for money, but the funding was helpful to get things started. Our small faithful group connected with LSM.

Building something new where there is a need has continued as a theme in my life.

Recently I took several self-assessments while working with Rozella Haydée White, my spiritual life coach. While learning about my particular gifts and limitations, I discovered that I am someone who creates and builds. I also realized that what comes naturally to me may not come naturally to other people. What works for me may not work for you. This was a helpful learning for me. It is probably not helpful for me to say to everyone who is looking for a campus ministry where there is none to just start their own. We're not all built the same way. We all have different contexts and different gifts. It takes patience and persistence to find your own path. It is good for me to remind myself that my path is not your path—it's my path.

Along my path, I had grown weary of being studied and discussed as a queer person in the ELCA, so I took a very large break from church.

MY FAMILY FINDS CALVARY

Fast-forward to 2009 when my family was attending St. Paul-Reformation Lutheran Church, one of very few ELCA congregations that had an out lesbian pastor.

When my wife and I had kids, we had started looking around for a suitable congregation and landed on St. Paul-Reformation Lutheran Church in St. Paul, Minnesota. Reverend Anita Hill was ordained and installed at St. Paul-Reformation in defiance of ELCA policy while I was on bedrest while pregnant with our first son. People traveled near and far to attend this queer-friendly church. It sounded like my kind of church! (Years later I had the privilege of mentoring Anita Hill when she started her real estate career!)

After the ELCA Churchwide Assembly's vote in 2009 allowing queer pastors in the ELCA, we felt comfortable in moving to another congregation. We appreciated St. Paul-Reformation, but we longed for a congregation that was more grounded in a community and closer to our home. We "church shopped" and were hoping for a congregation that was not only queer friendly but also had racial diversity.

We had visited Calvary previously when our dear friends Scott and Angie Endo had their children baptized. We decided to try out Calvary while the Endos were away in India for two years, because we wanted to like the church for the church, not just because our friends went there.

At Calvary we found a small community with a warm welcome, more racial diversity than most ELCA congregations, and relationships and activities that extended far beyond Sunday morning. Calvary had journeyed through the Reconciling in Christ process to welcome people of all sexual orientations and gender identities. Calvary had also called a pastor from the Extraordinary Ministries Roster, which was an alternate route for a queer candidate for ministry to get approved for a call and/or ordination.

One of the first things that drew me into Calvary was the women's group event called "A B.I.G. Night Out." B.I.G stood for "Beverage Interest Group" which meant that this group of women would go out together for happy hour. I appreciated happy hour as a way to get to know people. Going out to drink beer together was a signal to me that it was not a pretentious congregation and that relationships were important. We tried on Calvary for a while and eventually decided to join.

Facebook provided a helpful way for me to get to know members of Calvary. I was still getting to know Calvary member Felecia Boone when I saw her post on Facebook about her experience in traveling to the ELCA Churchwide Assembly in 2011. She said something like "I got a fro check when going through security, people are staring at me on this plane, and I know this is how it is going to be all week at Churchwide Assembly."

My heart just sank when I read these words because I knew that they were true and I knew how wrong it was. I was horrified when I realized that, in addition to people putting up with racism out in the world, they also had to put up with it in their church. This felt tremendously wrong to me. I felt a strong and unmistakable call to move my focus to racism in the church. I would eventually meet many Black and brown friends who shared with me their horrible experiences of racism and discrimination in the church. It is continually heartbreaking.

It was at Calvary that I first learned about harm done to brown and Black folks inside the church. It was also where I found a close community with relationships strong enough to engage in conversation about race.

Calvary members were involved in a massive "Vote No" campaign in Minneapolis in 2012 focused on defeating an amendment that would define marriage in the Minnesota constitution as being between one man and one woman. Then in 2013, we supported the passage of a law securing same-sex couples' right to marry. An organization called the Interfaith Roundtable was also very active in the "Vote No" campaign. When the "Vote No" campaign ended and same-sex couples gained the right to marry, the Interfaith Roundtable shifted its focus from same-sex marriage to racial justice. (This occurred around the time of Michael Brown being killed by police in Ferguson, Missouri, in 2014.) It was at this point that I was invited into the group. We eventually chose the name Multifaith Anti-Racism, Change, & Healing (MARCH) to reflect the new focus of the group.

MARCH has been a touchstone group for me over the years. I met a network of people deeply committed to doing racial justice work and worked alongside them. MARCH created and led many different valuable trainings and eventually created Sacred Solidarity, a multifaith cohort of congregational anti-racism groups. (As you'll learn in chapter 9, Calvary church as a whole later became involved with Sacred Solidarity.)

BEGINNING TO MARCH

In late 2013 I attended an anti-racism training for white activists led by people associated with MARCH. This training was transformative for me. At one point, one of the presenters asked the crowd "Who likes to get things really right before doing any anti-racist work?" My hand shot up along with everyone else's. "You have to stop that," the presenter said. **"You can't wait until you are perfect to act."** Later I would learn that perfectionism is a characteristic of white supremacy culture that serves to keep white supremacy in place. White folks have been fed that lie that we are supposed to be perfect, to make no mistakes. Perfectionism makes taking action difficult.

We were encouraged to show up and support brown- and Black-led organizations and leaders and to practice *followership*: just show up, listen, and follow the leadership of the brown and Black folks. I took this advice to heart and started showing up. I had to actively quiet the part of me that wanted to speak up and offer solutions.

What I learned when I started showing up to organizations and events led by brown and Black people was that folks who are in different situations are the experts on what they need and there are brilliant people everywhere. I don't need to come in with my idea of what a particular solution might be. I clearly remember being in a multiracial organizing space and I think I was the only white person in this breakout group. Everyone was saying the part they were going to play—what they were going to do. I said that I could tell white people to stop trying to control things and to just get out of the way. They all turned to me and said, "YEAH, WE NEED YOU TO DO THAT!" It's important to listen to community and to hear what community wants. I noticed that after I showed up again and again, trust started to develop. After trust develops, authentic relationships are possible. When you have authentic relationships, you can move together as beloved community.

When I was volunteering with one brown and Black organization on Election Day, we heard about some questionable actions occurring. A few of us wanted to check it out, so I offered to drive. I learned very quickly that I could not drive in the privileged way that I was used to. When I drove through a yellow light, the anxiety level in the car skyrocketed. I knew I needed to change my behavior to keep people safe. In a conversation in multiracial spaces about attending outside events, the question "Is it safe space for Black people?" came up. As someone who had been taught through the media and the world to be afraid of Black people, this was an important question for me to hear and an important dynamic for me to be aware of.

Being out in the world with brown and Black folks provides a very different window on the world than being out with other white folks. Things looked very different outside of my white bubble.

I did not previously think that I lived in a white bubble. I had a few brown and Black friends, my kids went to diverse schools, and we lived in a city that was multiracial. However, I had not really engaged with my brown and Black friends about race. I suspect that my relationships with Black and brown people at that time were likely not viewed by them as safe. Spending more time in multiracial spaces has helped me pop that white bubble and see the experiences of my friends. I know I can easily retreat to the bubble if I choose to, but that is not a faithful option.

In 2017 following the inauguration of the Donald Trump as the 45th president, massive Women's Marches were held all over the country, including

Saint Paul, Minnesota. I attended and was stunned at the sheer number of people who showed up. I had never seen a march of this size in Minnesota. I saw *many* people showing up at a march for the first time who seemed eager to make a difference. I also saw so many Black and brown friends angry and hurt that all of these people were just showing up now.

Where the hell had they all been when the protests were about the continued murder of Black and Indigenous people by police?

I suspected that all of these new folks showing up would have no idea about the anger felt by folks who had been abandoned for so many years. I was angry too. And. I didn't want to lose these new people who were just starting to show up who most likely had no clue about the anger felt by those wondering where this wave of new people had been. We needed these new people to stick with it. I decided I needed to do something. I had attended trainings for long enough. Maybe it was time for me to lead some trainings myself.

FOLLOWERSHIP AND WALKING HUMBLY

Amid my insomnia during early January 2017, I started envisioning a training curriculum in my mind when I was supposed to be sleeping.

I pitched the idea on Facebook—I would lead a training for white folks who were newly seeking to be anti-racist. The positive response was swift and encouraging, as I heard many versions of "Yes, please, please, please do this group." My brown and Black friends were exhausted and weary of teaching white folks. People were very concerned about what the new presidential administration would bring.

I sought a co-facilitator and was fortunate that my friend Katherine Parent said "yes" and brought her own racial justice journey and amazing artwork to the trainings.

Katherine and I have led the training several times since 2017, often in congregational settings. We designed the sessions for only white folks so that BIPOC people aren't harmed by the inevitable hurtful statements and actions that would likely occur. As someone drawn to being a protector, I explained to the white participants that if they said something harmful to a BIPOC person during the training, my inner velociraptor was likely to come out. I wanted white folks to be able to ask their questions and for me to be able to offer corrections without turning into a velociraptor. I wanted them to learn and to stay engaged.

Susan Raffo was one of the trainers at the 2013 activist training I had attended. During that and other events she has led, she talked about how deeply racism and white supremacy are embedded in our very bodies. I have learned that it is important to pay attention to what is happening in my body and what is happening with my emotions when dealing with issues of racism and white supremacy.

When I understand that I need to speak up and confront a racist comment, my throat tightens, urging me to be quiet. Often when I am starting to work on a project that involves dismantling white supremacy, my lips go numb and my body rebels against the work. I can find it harder to focus when writing about white supremacy or planning an anti-racism training than doing other types of work. It has been important for me to recognize these patterns in my body. Sometimes I have to metabolize these feelings of "frozenness" by hopping on the treadmill and going for a run. Sometimes I need to pause and listen to some music and move my body to reclaim it from the forces that want me to remain an accomplice to keeping white supremacy in place. Sometimes when I am feeling uneasy about something someone said and wondering if I should act, I hear whispers of "Well, are you really *sure* they meant something racist?" I also hear whispers of "Keep the peace—don't rock the boat." Moving my body has helped me shake off obedience to keeping quiet and maintaining the status quo.

Learning about white supremacy culture has also been invaluable in helping me understand characteristics of this culture in play. The Sacred Solidarity program of MARCH introduced people at Calvary to the White Supremacy Culture characteristics, a list developed by Tema Okun. I have found that having this list's fifteen characteristics spelled out has helped me to get a handle on white supremacy and to recognize and root it out of myself and institutions I am in contact with. I reference Tema Okun's article to this day (updated by the author in 2021 and available online at https://www.whitesupremacyculture.info). We begin every board meeting of EDLARJ with reviewing one of the characteristics of white supremacy culture, discussing how it lives in us and what we are using as antidotes to that characteristic. I am still learning, and I realize something new every time I engage with this work. Starting to let go of the white supremacy characteristic of "perfectionism" has been deeply liberating for me and made me a much happier person.

It was relatively easy for me to acknowledge my own personal racist thoughts, feelings, and actions once I was receptive to my own self-interrogation. But sometimes I still have trouble recognizing systemic racism. Unfortunately, even if we all pledged to be nicer people and eliminate racist thoughts from our minds, racist systems would still be in place and harm would still occur. We have to get at the systems to effect change.

Clearly systemic racism was at play in the Rockdale school system when they had different requirements for Black teachers. It was at play when my white family was able to get land but brown and Black folks could not.

Clearly systemic racism is present in the ELCA. Rev. Lenny Duncan writes about it extensively in *Dear Church: A Love Letter from a Black Preacher to the Whitest Denomination in the US*.

It would be a mistake to think that systemic racism was left in the past.

I felt convicted when I read *The New Jim Crow: Mass Incarceration in the Age of Colorblindness* by Michelle Alexander. Alexander discusses some of the systemic racism embedded in housing, including the use of credit scores as criteria for rental housing. My wife and I owned rental property for about fourteen years and at first did not recognize how using credit scores for tenant screenings had a racist component. Once we realized that it did, we decided that we could use other criteria for screening tenants.

The Fair Housing Act, which prohibits racial discrimination in housing, passed more than fifty years ago, yet discrimination in housing still exists. My real estate clients have taught me that they still face discrimination in getting mortgages, even when they have great credit scores and professional jobs. Some clients have had poor experiences with previous realtors. Many of my BIPOC clients carry trauma with them from past experiences with institutions and often have fear about the process. It is important for me to acknowledge their history and to connect them with lending partners and other professionals I know will treat them well and welcome all of their questions.

I was angry and unsurprised to learn about racial bias in house appraisals. When appraisers think that a home is owned by white people, they may appraise homes at a higher rate than when they think homes are owned by Black people. This is another instance of systemic racism that is important for me to be aware of. Recently when a client who is Black was preparing to have her house appraised, I talked with her about the racial bias in appraisals and how to navigate that bias. Together we decided on a plan. When phone calls were necessary, I would make the calls. My assistant who is white would be present while the appraiser was at the house to let them in and answer questions. She placed photos of white people around the home. It is hard to know if there would have been racial bias in this instance, but we ended up with an appraisal amount that I thought was fair.

I have learned far more from my relationships with people than I have from any book. When my relationships became more multiracial, it didn't take long for me to become friends with Black men who had been incarcerated. It broke my heart when a member from a Calvary family received a prison sentence that seemed way too long. It made no sense to me to pay all of that money to keep him locked up when he could have been home helping to care for his mother and other family members. The criminal justice system is full of systemic racism and racial disparities.

I am continually amazed and heartbroken by the ongoing instances of racial discrimination that my friends face in everyday life.

One thing I have noticed about myself is that I have not paid as much attention to the "walk humbly" part of Micah 6:8 compared with the other parts of the verse until fairly recently. I have learned that humility—walking humbly—is absolutely necessary in doing this work. The white supremacy characteristic of perfectionism has us believe that we can't make mistakes. White folks, let me tell you, we are going to make mistakes! Recognizing my own humanity and the reality that humans make mistakes has been liberating for me. Staying humble has been important.

Lastly, it has been important for me to understand the importance of taking on the posture of "accompaniment" or "journeying together" rather than as "white savior." Accompaniment requires listening and not assuming. The reality is that I need liberation from white supremacy too. We are all harmed, in different and unequal ways, by white supremacy.

The goal is collective liberation.

CHAPTER 9
WHY WAS CALVARY READY?

Calvary was ready to "meet the moment" after George Floyd was murdered because of the years of work we did on anti-racism and dismantling white supremacy, because Calvary is a close community with resilient relationships, and simply because of where we were located. We also had a pastor who understood that his place at this time was not to be front and center, but to run interference as needed.

When Pastor Hans Lee resigned from Calvary in January 2022, I gave him a photo of himself and a few Calvary members backstage at the concert by the artist Common as part of the first "Rise and Remember" commemoration of George Floyd's death. I explained that I experienced him as a "backstage pastor"—meaning that he had done a lot of work in the background and did not put himself center stage. This posture of Pastor Hans not being front and center *and* working in the background gave space for more Calvary people to step up into relationship with the community. It also helped pave the way for many of the bold things that we did.

When I had a conversation with Pastor Hans about what it was like to be pastor during the pandemic and during the uprising following the murder of George Floyd, I learned that being a "backstage pastor" was not his usual way of operating. But he knew that adaptation of his usual style was necessary. Here's how he explained it:

> I was willing to step in and be part and listen and encourage, and maybe sometimes run interference, but when George Floyd's murder took place, there were a number of people at Calvary that were able to step in in an appropriate way with the neighborhood. There were enough people at Calvary to step in and to be present and to listen to the neighborhood and be in that posture. I think you were kind of the leader of that. I didn't have to be, because you were doing it.

And when you say "the backstage pastor" . . . well, that's not really not my style—to be backstage. But in this case, it really is the right approach. Especially for a white pastor of an urban church, in a neighborhood that frankly is gentrifying, but also as this is going on, for me to be "front and center" would not have been appropriate at all, and I knew that right away.

The anti-racism work was driven by our congregational anti-racism team, the origins of which are a little fuzzy and uncertain. What is clear to me is that our success was dependent on strong relationships among individuals who recognized there was an urgent need for doing the work.

A marker for me of the development of Calvary's anti-racism team goes back to a Rally Sunday in 2011. I hosted a table for a book study on *The Grace of Silence* by Michele Norris (Vintage, 2011), a book about the author's experience as the first Black family on her block in a neighborhood near our church. Felecia Boone, a Black woman who grew up at Calvary and is a current Race Equity Committee member, hosted a table next to me at the same event. Felecia and I decided that we should work together after that Sunday. We ended up having a robust book study and discussion of *The Grace of Silence* with three different groups gathering in homes. The congregation seemed hungry for this kind of engagement and interaction.

Not everyone saw the relevance of discussing race in church. Scott Endo, who is Japanese American and a current Calvary Race Equity Committee member, recalls his initial uncertainty about reading a book that was not explicitly about church:

> I think there was some feeling at the beginning [of] "Is this appropriate to bring the book like the Michele Norris book that's not explicitly about church, but is about this neighborhood, and it's about an experience of the evolution of the neighborhood where Calvary is located?" To me that was part of it for me not having grown up in the church. I didn't really know what was like church and what wasn't. What I knew is that a book club around that wouldn't necessarily be something that naturally is part of church. So I didn't know any better, but it was asking "Is talking about this an appropriate thing to do? Does it feel like the right space for it?" I think four or five people said, "Why not? This seems like it has a lot of relevance."

Some people recall the anti-racism team being a "secret group," and others recall asking to join the group and being told that the group was closed—that there were other groups that could use some help. Since I tend to forge ahead, I was oblivious to these dynamics at the time. I was puzzled when I heard rumors of people not being able to be involved, because I wanted everyone to be involved. Others remembered the origins of our group as an informal, ad hoc group where people coalesced who were interested in exploring and talking about race in the church and race in general.

Felecia Boone knew that work was needed in our congregation in part because of how she felt as a member of the congregation. She shared in an interview that, while Calvary was going through a revisioning process where we proclaimed to be "radically welcoming," she didn't necessarily feel welcome:

I remember pulling the pastor aside and saying "I grew up in this church, and I do not always feel that radical welcome. I'm not telling you that to hold you hostage. I'm just telling you how I feel. So, if that is going to be a part of who Calvary says it is, it needs to factor in these things, because that's not always what I feel as a child of this congregation coming here."

I asked Felecia about what felt unwelcoming:

Did you feel that the talk wasn't expansive enough, or not aware enough, or that you weren't feeling welcome at the conversation? Did that have any anything to do with the kind of conversation that was going on, or the lack of talking about race and the conversation?

Felecia responded like this:

It was this statement that we are "radically welcoming." I'm part of this congregation and I don't feel radically welcomed, right? We spent time where we could securely take a vote of the congregation about whether or not we were going to become a Reconciling in Christ congregation, knowing that most likely it was going to pass and that we would lose some people. But most likely it was gonna pass, and it did, and we did lose some people. And yet race was the one place we weren't willing to spend time. So it's great that you're here and we love you, because we know you sort of kind of in some ways, even though there's some sideways shit happening right? And so I don't, in my adult years, always feel radically welcomed here. So I want us to address this "radically welcoming." What is that? What does that actually mean for us as a community?

For Calvary to be "radically welcoming," simply saying it did not and does not make it so. For Felecia and many others, being "radically welcoming" needed to include addressing race.

We worked as a Race Equity task force that planned several events such as book studies, intergenerational "fish bowl" conversations, movie nights, and temple talks that were personal stories about race. One memorable adult education was by Scott Endo's dad Todd Endo, who is the last living World War II member of the Japanese American Citizens League and who was present for the 1965 March on Washington for Jobs and Freedom.

The important thing is that we were having conversations about race in the church.

Another significant marker was the summer of 2015 when we spent an intensive summer focused on race. While our pastor took a three-month sabbatical, an interracial couple, Pastor Laura Ingersol, who is Black, and Pastor Jerrett Hansen, who is white, served as our pastors, guided us, and journeyed with us. The sermon each Sunday was focused on race, as were the book studies, movie nights, and discussions. For Star Trek fans, I describe this time as a "wormhole" in which we moved along the path of dealing with race faster than we normally would have due to the intensity of the summer's focus. Perhaps in 2015 this work was more easily done by someone other than a settled pastor. I was grateful for the time and excited to engage in rich conversation where some hearts were moved.

The year 2015 was also a time with a heavy amount of racial violence in the news, and the relevance of doing anti-racism work became more apparent for some. This is when Dylann Roof, a white Lutheran man, killed nine Black people in Emanuel African Methodist Episcopal Church, and when six Black churches in the south were burned.

Scott Endo discussed a shift in his perception of the relevance of addressing race at church:

> Then in 2015 there wasn't a question of whether there was relevance, because it was what was happening in the world, and we saw ourselves not looking inward only, but our place in the world as a church, and as a congregation and as Lutherans. I just remember that resonated a lot with me.

Not everyone was excited about the focus on race. Some people felt singled out, some people didn't appreciate the preaching, and some people took the summer off. However, many other people were grateful for the time.

Nancy Lee Nelson, former Race Equity Committee member now living abroad, shared this in an interview:

> Quite a few people were very thankful that Laura and Jerrett were there and attended the meetings, and wanted that to happen. Some people really took the time to be there and listen.

Felecia Boone added this:

> Even though it was hard, because there were people who said "This is not my comfort zone . . . and I'm learning."

Not everyone was on board though. Some people didn't appreciate Pastor Laura's and Pastor Jerrett's style. Former Race Equity Committee member Michael Weber recalled this:

> When Jerrett and Laura were there, we saw that there were some really passionately negative reactions.

One day in the midst of a discussion or announcements during worship, a Calvary member who was not part of formal leadership stood up and said, "I think we should put up a Black Lives Matter banner." I was ready to get a ladder and hang a sign that day! However, we had several members who had misgivings about such an action. I know that sometimes I act too quickly and that conversation and understanding are important, so I paused and participated in many discussions. It seemed helpful to have an outside person help us have conversations about a possible banner, so I invited my friend Denise Konen from First Universalist Church of Minneapolis to lead us in a discussion on why saying "all lives matter" is harmful and why saying "Black lives matter" is helpful.

Through all of the discussions, important learning happened and hearts and minds were moved. It was helpful for us as a congregation to really engage the conversation, instead of some people pretending they were okay with a decision and going along with the crowd. It brought time for more education, engagement, and understanding.

One of the tensions we hold as a Race Equity Committee is between waiting for everyone to be on board with us before taking action and moving ahead with action that is needed to decrease harm in the community or to move forward racial justice efforts.

Michael Weber, a Calvary member at the time, remembers much discussion about the banner:

> It wasn't just about the banner. It was "What does the banner say? How do we phrase the banner?" I remember the Church Council spent multiple meetings on whether or not we could just say "Black Lives Matter" versus "Black lives are sacred" or "All Black lives matter." We knew that just putting up a banner would never be enough, that there would need to be continued action to go along with a banner.

We eventually did decide to put up a Black Lives Matter banner, and the Sunday School children supported the effort by contributing the money they raised that year toward banner costs. I wondered if putting up the Black Lives Matter banner helped pave the way for relationship with our neighbors. When talking with a few longtime neighbors who were engaged at George Floyd

Square, I learned that people were more affected when we later put up the "In the City for Good" banner.

Marcia Howard, for example, recalls appreciating the play on words and the sentiment that the congregation wasn't going to flee the city and that the congregation was there to do "good things." Marcia signaled some skepticism about the "Black Lives Matter" sign. She recalled thinking "Let's see if they 'walk the walk.'" This echoes Felecia Boone's earlier thoughts on Calvary saying that we were "radically welcoming." It's not enough to just say it—action is needed.

At the end of their summer with us, Laura and Jerrett came up with recommendations for Calvary that included expanding our Race Equity group to up to eight members, making it an official standing committee, and tying our work to the mission of the church.

We worked to become an official committee at Calvary. Part of that process was bringing a resolution to our annual meeting to change our constitution to add the Race Equity Committee as a standing committee. There was some dissent. Some people felt it should just be a part of the social justice committee or a subcommittee. As Felecia Boone said, if it were a subcommittee, "it will be very easily subsumed into social justice, and then it won't be about race." We felt that it was important to have a standing committee that was specifically about race so that race was not put on the back burner as inevitably happens when there are other things to focus on.

Becoming a formally recognized Race Equity Committee showed that we were an important and more permanent part of the congregation. We weren't doing "special" work, but rather the work is a long-term commitment. Ad hoc groups are put together until they are no longer needed. The sad thing is there is no end in sight for the need to do racial justice work. Ad hoc is not going to work for an anti-racism team. We will spend our lives doing this work and never get to the end of it. Being on the journey is important, helps to move the needle, and is what being faithful looks like. Being a formal standing committee with a budget helps with the continuity of work. Budgets are moral documents that should include a commitment to racial justice work.

The Race Equity Committee has engaged in many different efforts. I was tempted to come up with a laundry list of *all* of the things that we have done, but I won't. Know that context is important and what works for Calvary may not work for other congregations. A couple of our overarching strategies were trying to reach and include as much of the congregation as possible and encouraging congregational decision-making through a race equity lens. Instead of my laundry list, I will just share just a few of the more notable things we have done.

As I've mentioned, in 2016 we joined Sacred Solidarity. This is a multi-faith cohort of congregational anti-racism teams organized by Multifaith Anti-Racism, Change, & Healing (MARCH). MARCH decided that each group should use whatever process made sense in the polity of each congregation to get approval to join the Sacred Solidarity cohort. For Calvary we thought it made sense to get the approval from the church council. We naively expected it would be an easy process. We experienced some resistance because of the concerns of a few council members. Some people expressed discomfort around stark talk about white supremacy culture. Some people showed concerns about connecting with a group outside Calvary, claiming it would be distracting. We knew that our work in this cohort would mean we would still need to center the needs of people of color, not what the white people in these groups thought was needed. We invited a Unitarian Universalist pastor and a United Church of Christ pastor to talk with our church council, and eventually the council agreed that we could join Sacred Solidarity.

It was helpful to connect with other congregations engaged in the work. The work that we did on white supremacy culture was deeply transformational.

Scott Endo shared about his experience:

I remember that the language of white supremacy culture was really super helpful for me for framing how you could talk about white supremacy and when you encounter the hackles that go up. My reaction at the beginning also was that [hackles raising occurs] because white supremacy culture carries a certain connotation which has to do with white supremacists and what that looks like.

I think the idea of white supremacist culture and the idea of "It's the air we breathe" or "It's the water and we are the fish and we don't realize the water is there" was really helpful as a tool to be able to talk with people or feel prepared to talk with people. It helped to get through the automatic reaction of feeling defensive or feeling it's personalized or feeling "It's so extreme." It's helpful to talk about culture, and how we uphold culture. To talk about how we live in it and how we can either recognize it and do something or recognize it and not do something about it. You can continue to uphold it and benefit from it or actively counter it. The idea that it is not about just you precisely was very eye opening. I felt like it gave me language and a framework that was easy for actually having conversation in all parts of my life.

Felecia Boone responded to Scott with how it is helpful to look at things in an institutional or systemic way. I found this response personally helpful and want to share it here:

Scott, that's a helpful thing, because that's how we frame it in my work for county employees. People get stuck in individual acts of racism instead of looking at systems, institutions, and how systems operate. So the place we have the least opportunity to make change is at the individual level, but if we bring it up to the systemic level, that's where we can look at our policies, practices, procedures to say, what is the policy around calling for backup on a traffic stop? Is it everybody just hears it on the radio so everybody goes there, or do we have a policy about how you respond to certain traffic stops? What are the policies that allow the people's individual prejudices? How do we put some guardrails around these things, so that individual prejudices aren't at play in the decision making?

We did significant work with the Intercultural Development Inventory (IDI) and Intercultural Development Plan (IDP). The IDI is a survey that assesses intercultural competence at both an individual and an organizational level. The IDP is an individualized plan for increasing cultural competence.

We were able to connect and work with qualified administrators (QAs) of the IDI through the Minneapolis Area Synod. We followed their suggestion of a tiered approach in which we first had the Race Equity Committee, then church council, and finally interested members of the congregation take the IDI inventory. Individuals then reviewed their results with their QA and received their IDP. The three groups also received reports on their results as a group and a plan for improvement.

We heard that many people and institutions don't end up doing much with their IDI results and IDP, partially because some people are offended by where they fall on the continuum and assume that the tool must be flawed. Also, sometimes it's just hard to do things alone. Because we felt that the work was important and because we wanted to be good stewards of the investment we made in the IDI, we implemented a process of allocating part of church council meetings and REC meeting to do IDP homework together. We also created many group experiences which enabled people to do IDP homework together. We plan to revisit IDI and IDP work.

Each quarter we invited a BIPOC person to preach and teach at Calvary. We felt it was important for people to hear the voices of BIPOC folks from the pulpit, and these guest preachers moved people. Because we know that additional emotional labor is involved for a BIPOC person to preach and teach in a predominantly white congregation, we pay them more than our standard rate. We have been richly blessed by this amazing preaching and teaching.

We had a couple intergenerational "fishbowl" conversations that allow any participants to enter the center of a circular discussion group. One involved creating a race timeline for the city, the country, and Calvary, with youth asking questions of elders. The second one involved youth asking questions of elders and beyond about the differences between civil rights movement 1.0 (during the 1960s) and civil rights movement 2.0 (current time). Members seemed to *love* these conversations.

We also marched and showed up for protests.

We invited Calvary members to share their personal stories related to race as temple talks.

We have done several book studies, including *The Cross and the Lynching Tree* by Rev. Dr. James H. Cone, *America's Original Sin: Racism, White Privilege, and the Bridge to a New America* by Jim Wallis, *The Watsons Go to Birmingham—1963* by Christopher Paul Curtis, and *Dear Church* by Rev. Lenny Duncan. About six different groups were reading *Dear Church* together when the pandemic hit. Groups meeting at homes worked well for us pre-pandemic.

Calvary's study of *The Cross and the Lynching Tree* was particularly helpful to me in theologically framing our position at Calvary. In February 2017, Dr. Mary Lowe helped to start Calvary's study of the book *The Cross and the Lynching Tree* by Rev. Dr. James H. Cone, founder of Black Liberation Theology. Dr. Lowe asked us to consider the perspectives of the different people present at Jesus' lynching: those who called for the execution of Jesus, the Roman Empire, bystanders, and supporters of Jesus.

If we consider ourselves followers of Jesus, we need to reflect on who we are in the story today.

If we are followers of Jesus, we can't call for his execution, we can't support the unjust systems of empire, and we can't be bystanders.

If we are to be followers of Jesus, we must be in solidarity with the oppressed and work for justice.

If we are to be followers of Jesus, we must follow the example that he set for us. We need to be careful and keep asking ourselves about who Jesus was, because white supremacy works to distort the image of Jesus in the service of empire. White supremacy has us put up stained glass images of white Jesus— Jesus who in reality was a brown-skinned Palestinian Jewish man who stood with marginalized people and was executed by the state at Calvary.

For me, being part of a church called Calvary one block from where George Floyd was lynched and being faithful means working with our neighbors for justice and collective liberation. It means staying, rolling up our sleeves, and getting to work. This study had a significant impact on preparing me to meet the moment of George Floyd's lynching a block from my church.

Throughout the years we have also intentionally spent social time together as a committee, including going on a couple of weekend retreats. Having strong relationships with good tensile strength is important when doing anti-racism work, because the work is hard and you need support to continue in the work.

I spoke with Pastor Hans Lee about Calvary's readiness to meet the moment when the uprising happened. He had this to say:

> I had served two congregations that had significant membership of people of color in Milwaukee and in Minneapolis, but when I got to Calvary it was such a different vibe, I think, because of the work that you guys were doing trying to keep this issue of white supremacy in the church front and center. I think one of the things that I learned from you especially and others as well was that this is white people's work and that Calvary—at least some people at Calvary—were taking that very seriously.

> I think Calvary was in some ways in a better position to deal with something like the George Floyd [murder] than other congregations I've served, but I can't say that for sure, because it was such a unique experience, and so awful. It's hard, because the congregation didn't fully rally, let's be honest. It's impossible to talk about this without also talking about the pandemic, because the pandemic created a situation in which a lot of people at Calvary . . . a number of families kind of checked out during the pandemic. So when George Floyd happened in the midst of that, it was a number of really talented people that knew how to step in. The IDI, the racial equity work that you were doing that goes back to 2015. **All of that gave a core group of people the right frame of mind to step into this in a way that was about accompaniment, and not about leading.**

> I think what Calvary had in its DNA, at least among those who did show up, was the ability to listen.

CHAPTER 10
WHAT'S NEXT

———

The presumptive audience for this chapter is white ELCA Lutherans. The whole reason I am writing this book is because I want you and your congregation to get ready to meet the moment when the next George Floyd is murdered near your church. Beyond that, I want you to join me and others in making the church a less harmful place to be and for you to be actively anti-racist in church and society.

It takes a lot of work and we will never finish the job, but we have to act. We have to. Our baptismal promises compel us to act by renouncing evil and caring for our BIPOC siblings in Christ who are being killed and harmed at alarming rates. When part of the body hurts, we all hurt. Jesus shows us by word and deed that we are to side with the marginalized and oppressed. My favorite Bible verse, my *cantus firmus* Micah 6:8—"And what does the LORD require of you but to do justice, and to love kindness, and to walk humbly with your God?"—clearly calls us to act justly. Our siblings Kenneth Wheeler in *US: The Resurrection of American Terror* and Lenny Duncan in *Dear Church: A Love Letter From a Black Preacher to the Whitest Denomination in the U.S.* both clearly call on white folks in the church to take up the work of anti-racism and fighting white supremacy.

Fair warning—when you open up your heart to understanding the harm done to BIPOC folks in our country and in our church, your heart will get broken. Repeatedly. It's the cost of regaining your humanity that has been taken from you by conforming to white supremacy culture. It's the cost of discipleship.

Here are some specific ideas for how you can do this:

1. Find other white people to talk with about race, anti-racism, and dismantling white supremacy, making sure this work centers around the input of BIPOC people, especially those in your church and community.

It is also important to acknowledge that engaging in conversations about race with white people can take a lot of emotional labor for BIPOC folks. So talk with other white folks. These people could be your friends, your pastor, an existing anti-racism group in your church, or groups such as Showing Up for Racial Justice (SURJ). They could be connected with the European Descent Lutheran Association for Racial Justice (EDLARJ).

Unfortunately, many white folks have not developed their "talking about race" muscles, and we can tire out pretty quickly in conversations. This just isn't acceptable any more. We need to develop the capacity for talking about race and having hard conversations. Also, dismantling white supremacy and becoming anti-racist is hard! It is impossible to do this work alone—you are going to need support from, at the very least, one friend.

2. Remember your baptism.

We are all baptized into one body, the body of Christ. When one member hurts, we all hurt. We are in it together and need to care for one another. Our baptismal promises call us to renounce evil and work for justice.

3. Think about who Jesus was, the example he gave, and what he called us to do.

When we don't critically think about Jesus, it can be easy to fall into the idea that he was this pleasant white guy who is depicted in many of our stained glass windows at church. Jesus flipped tables, and he was killed by the state for standing up for his friends. Again and again Jesus calls us to be with marginalized people.

We rarely talk about *kenosis* and Jesus and the ways that Jesus continually gave up power and ultimately his very life on the cross. I'm just a street theologian, but I don't often hear people talk about the "giving up power" part of following Jesus. White folks, if people are going to be moved out of the margins, if we are going to stop marginalizing people, we have to get out of the middle. We have to de-center ourselves—we have to give up power.

4. Start to gain an understanding of white supremacy culture and how it lives in you.

Next, start to root white supremacy culture out of yourself. In Chapter 9, Scott Endo talks about how it is helpful to think about white supremacy culture as "the air that we breathe" or "it's water and we are the fish" rather than it being about individual white supremacists. It can be *very* easy to not see white supremacy culture at play. If we don't actively examine white supremacy culture at work, we participate in it and help to keep it in place without realizing it.

As Scott Endo said, *"It's helpful to talk about culture, and how we uphold culture. To talk about how we live in it and how we can either recognize it and do something or recognize it and not do something about it. You can continue to uphold it and benefit from it or actively counter it."* I have found Tema Okun's work on the characteristics of white supremacy culture to be extraordinarily helpful.

5. Lean into your Lutheran roots and theology.
There are so many great things about Lutheran theology that support doing anti-racism work!

The white supremacy characteristic of "perfectionism" whispers to us that we need to do more or be better before we start an anti-racism book study at church. Perfectionism can send us down a spiral of shame if we are accused of being racist and can make us a little fragile. Perfectionism says we need to be more sure before we confront someone. It whispers "you might make a mistake."

You can shout back! "As a Lutheran I know I am saved by grace and I am simultaneously saint and sinner. Because I am saved by grace, I am freed by Christ to go ahead and do work in the world. Martin Luther's most important thing is care for neighbors and that is what I am doing when I do anti-racism work. I know it's going to be messy and I am going to make mistakes, but guess what, forces of evil? We believe in the priesthood of *all* believers. It's not just our pastors who are forever marked with the cross of Christ—it is *all* baptized believers."

6. Drop the white savior mode and assume a posture of accompaniment, especially if you want to engage more with your community.
Confession time again—I have definitely been in "white savior" mode before and can sometimes slip into it. I remember thinking "I should really go over to the north side (of Minneapolis) and read to those kids." And when in college, "I should teach people who use the food shelf about complementary proteins." My intentions were good—but both of these proclamations were made in the absence of relationship. I hadn't had a single conversation with any of the people involved that I may want to help, and I know that BIPOC people are the experts on their own experiences.

My friend Dr. Kelly Sherman-Conroy has shared how awful it was to have people show up at Pine Ridge Reservation, do some random work, and just leave. I see many examples of people trying to help without being in the context of relationship and the efforts fail. People often bring food to George Floyd Square and just leave it there. Without someone to receive the food it frequently goes bad. One time someone ordered eighty pizzas to be delivered to Holy Trinity during the intense food distribution time. I am sure this was well intentioned, but without someone to manage the pizzas or knowing whether anyone wanted pizza, it became a burden.

We saw some good examples of accompaniment from the Calvary food shelf. For me, accompaniment is not just about my journeying with someone else. It is us journeying together and listening to one another.

7. Make space for grief and lament for the harm done to BIPOC people.

When we make space for grief and lament, we honor it and the people being harmed. When there are instances of harm in your community or the news, include prayers and sermons about it in your service. All too often we want to skirt difficult topics and emotions and keep things happy. "Right to comfort" is another entrenched characteristic of white supremacy culture. White folks, we need to give up being comfortable and recognize the pain and grief. If someone comes to you with their grief and pain—listen. Making space for grief can also help to open your heart.

8. Start or join an anti-racism team in your congregation.

If you can only find one other person, start with one other person. The important thing is to start talking and thinking about race. I highly recommend *Faithful Steps: A Step-by-Step Guide for Congregations Starting to Engage in Racial Justice* compiled by Brenda Blackhawk. One misstep we made with the Calvary Race Equity Committee was not explicitly inviting enough seniors. Be sure to invite seniors and invite youth too.

9. Read!

My book suggestions include these titles:

> *Waking Up White: and Finding Myself in the Story of Race* by Debby Irving (Elephant Room Press, 2014)
> *Pre-Post-Racial America: Spiritual Stories from the Front Lines* by Sandhya Rani Jha (Chalice Press, 2015)
> *The New Jim Crow: Mass Incarceration in the Age of Colorblindness* by Michelle Alexander (The New Press, Tenth Anniversary Edition, 2020)
> *Baptized in Tear Gas: From White Moderate to Abolitionist* by Elle Dowd (Broadleaf Books, 2021)
> *America's Original Sin: Racism, White Privilege, and the Bridge to a New America* by Jim Wallis (Brazos Press, 2016)

> *The Cross and the Lynching Tree* by James H. Cone (Orbis Books, 2011)
> *Emergent Strategy: Shaping Change, Changing Worlds* by adrienne maree brown (AK Press, 2017)
> *The Watsons Go to Birmingham—1963* by Christopher Paul Curtis (Delacorte, 1995; several later editions also available)
> *My Grandmother's Hands: Racialized Trauma and the Pathway to Mending Our Hearts and Bodies* by Resmaa Menakem (Central Recovery Press, 2017)
> *Caste: The Origins of Our Discontents* by Isabel Wilkerson (Random House, 2020)
> *US: The Resurrection of American Terror* by Kenneth W. Wheeler (Precocity Press, 2022)
> *Dear Church: A Love Letter from a Black Preacher to the Whitest Denomination in the U.S.* by Lenny Duncan (Fortress Press, 2019)

Lastly, you could read the *Living Lutheran* article "Unpacking White Privilege: The Important Work of Making the Church Less Harmful" that I and Rev. Dr. Yolanda Denson-Byers wrote. You can find it by searching online for the article title.

10. Show up to an organization led and run by BIPOC folks.

Listen and support the BIPOC groups. (If you have trouble finding one, check with the NAACP or with a local predominantly BIPOC congregation.) After you get a sense of some of the organization's needs through relationships with members of the organization, create a list of things your congregation may be able to assist with.

11. Learn about the racial history of the place you live, your church, and your family.

What tribe(s) lived and still live on the land your church sits on? What was going on in your town in the 1960s? Did the schools integrate? Did you have family members who fought on both sides of the Civil War like I did? Understanding who you are and where you came from helps you enter into relationships with more clarity and intention.

12. Find your place in the work for racial justice.

We all have different gifts, and there are many different roles to play. What is right for me and my church may not be right for you and your church. Everyone has a role to play, and everyone *has* to play a role. If you want to jump start things, you can work with a coach. I have had a great experience working with Rozella Haydée White as my coach. I chose to do assessments to help reveal my strengths and weaknesses and to focus on how I could be a more effective leader. Be prayerful, patient, and persistent, and you will find your spot.

13. Stay humble and curious.

Chances are good that just like I did some pretty racist things when I was at Camp Lone Star without realizing it, you are doing racist things and causing harm without meaning to. Sadly our ELCA congregations are full of instances of harm being done to BIPOC siblings—I believe that much of it is done unintentionally. Ask yourself if your congregation is doing more to hold up white supremacy or to live out the gospel. Look around your church and notice what images of Jesus look like. How are "black" and "white" used as imagery in your hymns?

If you are fortunate to get some feedback from BIPOC siblings about the harm they are experiencing, listen with a spirit of humility and be curious about the thoughts you have, the feelings you feel in your body, and the emotions that arise. For example, "My throat feels tight and I am feeling defensive. I wonder why that is." Racism and white supremacy live deeply in our bodies. When a threat to us is perceived, such as being called out for saying something racist, a part of our brain that deals with emotions, especially fear, the amygdala, can get overly activated and render us incapable of clear thinking. We may even start to cry and become defensive. We need to be curious and aware about what happens with our bodies and emotions. We need to learn how to calm down our fearful brains for the sake of the gospel. Resmaa Menakem has written extensively about somatic experiences in *My Grandmother's Hands*. I recommend spending some time with this book.

14. Be aware of the effect of showing up in a white body in multiracial spaces.

Let's be honest, there has been a very long and continued history of white folks causing harm to BIPOC people. Showing up in a white body often means that you are a potential threat to them that, at a minimum, needs to be assessed. We have this history of not being aware of our racists acts, becoming emotionally dysregulated when confronted, and centering ourselves in conversation. The conversations that can happen in the room among BIPOC folks are disrupted when white folks show up.

When an event is advertised as Black-only or BIPOC-only, respect that boundary—even if you want to show up with good intentions to "just listen." How is your amygdala doing right now? Take some breaths. Hear me when I tell you that this does not mean that we need to live segregated lives. What I am saying is to be aware of the effect of your white body on BIPOC people. What

I have *been* saying is that we need to journey together in relationship with one another. This means not making assumptions, but showing up and listening.

15. Rebuild the foundation.

On page 16 of *Caste: The Origins of Our Discontents,* author Isabel Wilkerson describes America as an old house. I love that metaphor for thinking about our country. She discusses the tendency to not want to face the problems of an old house: "When you live in an old house, you may not want to go into the basement after a storm to see what the rains have wrought. Choose not to look, however, at your own peril. The owner of an old house knows that whatever you are ignoring will never go away. Whatever is lurking will fester whether you choose to look or not. Ignorance is no protection from the consequences of inaction."

Wilkerson discusses how no one alive today was around when America was built. People frequently want to distance themselves from sins of the past by saying things like "My family never owned slaves" or "My family never attacked Indigenous people." So while we may not have been around when the racist systems or caste systems were put into place, we inherited "the house," and things aren't going to get better until we take a look and address the foundation. There is no quick fix! It is going to take a lot of work, and we are going to have to work together.

This difficult, joyful, messy work of being actively anti-racist and dismantling white supremacy is impossible to do alone. It is necessary to labor with others—so join with others. If you take time for prayer and space for discernment, the Spirit will show up. God will be with you on this journey. I will be cheering you on.

ACKNOWLEDGMENTS

I give thanks to God from whom all blessings flow. Without abundant grace from God and from many people, I would not have been able to open my heart and interrogate my past.

I am grateful to Rev. Dr. Yolanda Denson-Byers who invited me to write an article with her for *Living Lutheran* magazine. I had zero idea how writing for any sort of publication worked. Yolanda forged ahead, encouraged me, and helped me to write in my own voice. We were both surprised when our article ended up on the cover of *Living Lutheran*. (I fully expected them to tell us to cut our article in half and for it to be placed in the back of the magazine.) After this article was published, we were asked to write for a couple of other publications and discovered that we have a lot to say. Writing a book is not something that was previously on my radar. Writing with Yolanda changed that.

I have been blessed to be a part of the community at George Floyd Square. While many people were feeling isolated during the beginning of the global pandemic, I was intensely connected with people in the Square. They cared enough about me to confront any nonsense from me, and they called when they didn't see me for a few days. The care that is shown for community members is astounding and the best example of the beloved community I have ever seen. As I write this, we are close to the three-year mark of George Floyd's murder, and the meetings, the community, the care, and the work for justice continue. I am eternally grateful. No justice, no streets.

I am grateful for the Calvary community that extends way beyond who shows up for worship on Sunday mornings. Special thanks to members of the Race Equity Committee and everyone who showed up to do the work.

It mattered.

It made a difference.

It made it possible for us to go outside and be transformed by the neighbor and by the moment.

I have abundant gratitude for my Black, Indigenous, Asian, Latiné, Arab, and Middle Eastern friends who have been generous and patient in their conversations with me. Thank you for your trust and helping me on my journey towards collective liberation.

Abundant gratitude for all of the people who graciously agreed to be interviewed for this book. You really made the book.

A big thank you to my real estate assistant Anna Tracy, who truly helps me do all of the things.

My amazing editor, Dawn Rundman, demystified the process of writing a book and made it accessible for me. She remained patient and encouraging and prioritized letting my voice come through. Thank you. I definitely could not have done it without you.

Lastly, I offer thanks to my North Star, my wife Melissa. She questions me, supports me, and loves me. I gratefully receive. I love you babe.

ABOUT THE AUTHOR

Shari Seifert is bi-vocational. She helps people buy and sell houses as a realtor and she dismantles white supremacy in the (ELCA) Lutheran church. Shari currently serves as president of the European Descent Lutheran Association for Racial Justice (EDLARJ) and is a member of Calvary Lutheran Church and part of the community at George Floyd Square. She lives, plays, and works in Minneapolis on land that was forcibly taken from the Dakota people.